Premier R̶e̶l̶e̶a̶s̶e̶ ̶C̶o̶m̶m̶e̶n̶ts

"I found the story to be compelling and moving. I cannot imagine the strength needed to write such a powerful story, let alone withstand such a period of heartache, pain, and ultimately, redemption."

Shawna Chambliss

"I believe those who read this story will find inspiration and the faith that we all so desperately need at certain points in our life to overcome adversity."

Linda Carter

"A 'birds-eye-view' into the world of domestic violence, insightful and touching."

Mary Waln

"This story brings to the forefront the cycle of abuse that women everyday go through. Darlene shows us the power of God in her life. The characters are real; you feel like you are right there."

Laurie Schulke

Don't Die for Love

Escape the Cycle of Violence

D.F.D. Nance

Order this book online at www.trafford.com
or email orders@trafford.com

Most Trafford titles are also available at major online book retailers.

The purpose of this book is to inspire those who
are in unhealthy relationships to make a change

Illustrator: Deborah M. De la torre
FOREWORD: Eva Howard MSW LCSW LSCSW
Editor: Deborah Shouse

Printed in the United States of America.
Published by Darlene Dunn Nance.
Printed by the Copy Club, April 2007.

The Copy Club, 9095 Bond, Overland Park, KS 66214

For more copies of this book send email to: loveisfree0@yahoo.com

ISBN: 978-1-4269-4444-4 (sc)
ISBN: 978-1-4269-4442-0 (hc)
ISBN: 978-1-4269-4443-7 (e)

Library of Congress Control Number: 2010914948

Our mission is to efficiently provide the world's finest, most comprehensive book publishing
service, enabling every author to experience success. To find out how to publish your book,
your way, and have it available worldwide, visit us online at www.trafford.com

Trafford rev. 10/29/2010

Trafford
PUBLISHING®   www.trafford.com

North America & international
toll-free: 1 888 232 4444 (USA & Canada)
phone: 250 383 6864 • fax: 812 355 4082

Dedication

All honor and praise be unto God, and my Lord Jesus Christ, who is my Savior.

I dedicate this book to my children Bradrell, Hanslee III, and Joshua, who gave me joy to see them grow and a reason to live and write this book; to my sister, Loretta, who was there for me when I needed help with anything; to my mother, Ethel, and brother, Keith, who always gave me encouragement when I needed it.

I also dedicate this book to all the women who are being abused and to all those who have escaped the cycle of violence.

Special Thanks

I want to say thanks to the following people:

Deborah Shouse, my editor, who, I believe, was sent by God to help me with making my dream come true;

Karen Boyd, my sister in Christ, who I also believe was sent by God to proofread my book;

Deborah M. De la Torre, my illustrator, who created the art work for my book cover;

Eve Howard MSW LCSW LSCSW, my therapist and spiritual advisor (she was/is to me like Samuel was to Saul, but unlike Saul, I was obedient), who wrote my Foreword;

Carrol Garrett, my friend, co-worker and the first person who said I inspired her with my story;

My premier readers, who volunteered to read my book and gave me feedback before it was published.

Table of Contents

FOREWORD

Abuse is defined as the subjugation of one person over another; the forms of abuse are verbal, emotional, sexual, physical, economic, psychological, stalking and spiritual abuse. Many women do not realize they are being abused until they enter counseling; they enter counseling because they feel depressed. Since there was no hitting, they didn't realize they had abuse issues.

Every 15 seconds a woman is beaten in the United States. It seems as though we live in a country that has declared war on women and children. Across the nation, women are entering the homes of friends or family, domestic violence shelters, emergency rooms, doctors' offices, substance abuse treatment programs, and even prison as a result of attempting to cope with domestic violence by an intimate partner. Many women take their children and leave the abusive environment, only to return time and time again, succumbing to the promises of their intimate partner that it will "never happen again." But of course, it does happen again and again and again, sometimes ending in serious injury, severe emotional breakdown (requiring psychiatric treatment) and, in extreme cases, death. A major aspect of domestic violence is the children growing up in these homes. We know a boy raised in an abusive home is more likely to become a batterer, and a girl raised in the same environment is more likely to become a victim. The children do not have a choice or voice in the violent household. The abusive environment has devastating effects on children: absenteeism from school, aggression with siblings, teachers, or peers, substance abuse, depression, attention deficit disorder (a common diagnosis seen in children of women living in abuse), low self-esteem and involvement in the criminal justice system.

Those of us who work in domestic violence teach the cycle of violence to women in abusive relationships: *tension building, the explosion or incident, and the honeymoon phase.* Even though this explains why women stay and continue to return to the abuse, remaining free of violence is more complicated than learning the cycle. **It requires a strong gut-wrenching, soul-searching desire to live in peace and a belief that one's life can change even if it means being alone.** Many do not believe their life can be different, because of painful unresolved childhood issues that have seared their very soul, poor social support systems, limited skills in the job market, poor credit histories, and lack of financial resources, not to mention low self-esteem. I've heard many women in unhealthy relationships facing the reality that she has to overcome these barriers, say she feels overwhelmed and wants to simply throw in the towel, repeating the cycle her mother, grandmother, or aunts lived. Unhealthy relationships can be with men who are "womanizing," lazy, irresponsible, egotistical, abusive, unsupportive, narcissistic, spiritually bankrupt and simply needy.

The study of human behavior teaches us that people have certain needs that must be met: physical, emotional, social, intellectual, and spiritual. Most people will attempt to meet all their other needs except the spiritual...they very often utilize people, food, addictions (gambling, etc.), money and many other things in place of spiritual fulfillment. Even though they are on a journey to self fulfillment, they find little peace or direction without a relationship with God. Many recovering addicts will report feeling lost, entering treatment programs that help provide tools for change, but they could not stay sober until they understood God's plan for their life.

Darlene, at a very young age, developed a desire to know God's word. After trying over and over to escape the horror she lived with her husband, she made a decision to turn her will over to God and do it His way. The 12-step program for alcoholics anonymous has been successful for over fifty years. Even though she did not have any substance abuse issues, she utilized many of the same tools recovering people use: the 3rd step talks about "turning our will and our lives over to the care of God" as we understand Him. Step 11 involves praying. Darlene credits her relationship with the Holy Spirit as one of intimacy: hearing His voice, experiencing His presence and comfort that ultimately changed her life. Once she began depending on God for guidance, she was able to move toward being whole. She found the answers in prayer, worship, and reading the Word of God. Many times prayer during our counseling sessions gave her the direction she needed. She is an example of a woman who was sick and tired of being sick and tired.

Darlene was like a "sponge," absorbing everything she could to promote a violence-free life and the peace that comes only when surrendering to God. Her book is very clear, concise and to the point for anyone who reads it. It is a roadmap to recovery for those hoping to embrace change. Darlene developed a strong desire for change in her life and the lives of her three children. Her children were especially important in her decision to leave her abusive relationship with her husband.

Often clergy will tell a wife who is being battered to "keep praying, your husband will change." However, God first deals with a man's will, but the man has to furnish the will to change. Her story points out the need for individuals to take responsibility for their lives and realize that mistakes or misuse in the past do not have to determine one's future. Most importantly there will be little change until one seeks God.

Eva Howard, MSW LCSW LSCSW

Eva Howard, MSW LCSW LSCSW, is the therapist for Newhouse, a domestic violence shelter in Kansas City, Missouri; she also runs a small private practice. Ms Howard has a multifaceted background in the field of social work. She has done group facilitation in psychiatric facilities; contracted with Children's Mercy Hospital TIES program, counseling women in recovery; and served as a consultant for the University of Kansas School of Social Welfare-

Community Transitions Project, a joint venture between the Kansas State Department of Corrections and the University of Kansas (providing services for people on parole). She is an affiliate of Social Work PRN. She especially enjoys presenting seminars on domestic violence and ethics. Ms Howard is also a licensed minister. Her greatest strength is giving people hope in spite of their circumstance.

Dear Reader,

First, I want to give thanks to God for saving me from the one I love. As I look back over my life, I wasted many, many years wishing and hoping for a man to love me just as much as I loved him. I realized though, I shouldn't let my past dictate my future. I am proud to say, I have gotten past those wasted years and have started making positive decisions in my life. The only part I will never regret is the birth of my children; I love them with all my heart. Second, I thank God for the ability to forgive my abuser. I have forgiven him and wish him well.

I'm grateful I decided not to "Die for Love." I share my story because I want to send a message that no one has to "Die for Love." My advice to all who are in unhealthy relationships is to *live for love*. Stop making excuses and make plans to escape the cycle of violence, NOW! It is okay to care about the father/mother of your child/children from a distance, but accept the reality that being in a relationship with him/her could destroy you. Live for the love you have in your heart from God, the Creator; live for your family, friends, and even your enemies, but from a distance. Someone is out there waiting to share their true love with you, the kind of love that involves care, respect, knowledge and responsibility. Most of all live for the love you have for yourself.

Again, I encourage you to "*Live for Love*."

November 27, 2001

Introduction

Baton Rouge, Louisiana, known as just another sleepy river town, was the place I called home for 34 years. It was a lovely, quiet place to live. When I was young, I didn't know I was poor because all my basic physical needs were met. I never went hungry a day of my young life. I always had clean clothes and shoes to wear. I had decent shelter where I lived with my maternal grandmother, along with my mother, my sister, my brother, and two of my cousins in a one-bedroom shot gun house. My grandmother's house had the kitchen on one end, the living room with a front porch attached on the other, and the bathroom and bedroom in the middle. When it was time to sleep my grandmother made sure all of us were comfortable, even though we had to share three beds and two couches. I can remember never wanting to grow older than ten. I had so much fun and not a care in the world.

I loved going to school, even though we had to walk three miles to get there. Elementary school was fun because I loved learning new and exciting things. When I was in the fifth grade, I wrote my first book and it was about my sister, my brother and me. "Why We Have to Fight All the Time" was the name of the book. My book was about how my mother was never home and how my sister, my brother and I were always fighting with each other, and how I wished we wouldn't fight so much.

Being outdoors is another one of my enjoyable memories. I liked going outside in my bare feet and I got into some trouble for liking it so much. We had an elder cousin who warned us about going outside without shoes. He said that we could cut our feet on a piece of glass or get a nail stuck in it. If he caught us outside without our shoes on he'd threaten us with a spanking. I didn't think it could happen to me so I continued sneaking outside in my bare feet. Then it happened, I cut my foot badly on a piece of glass and had to get several stitches. After that incident, I understood why my elder cousin told me that for my own good. He cared for us kids like we were his own, and he didn't want to see us get hurt. He didn't have any children of his own. He made us laugh with his jokes every time we saw him and sometimes he'd have candy or cookies for us.

Junior high and senior high school weren't so much fun. There was a boy I really liked in junior high, but I don't think he liked me. One day after school I was walking down the sidewalk that led out of the school, when I saw the boy I liked. I looked at him and smiled and I guess he didn't like it. He came up to me and told me not to look at him, but I told him that I could look at whomever I wanted. Then he hit me and we started fighting until a teacher came out and broke up the fight. That's about the only memory I have of my two years in junior high.

In high school almost all the guys made fun of me. I didn't let them bother me; I just focused on my studies so that I could graduate. When I was in the tenth grade, there was one guy in high school I thought was very handsome and wanted to get to know. I wrote him a note asking him to meet me after school in the football bleachers, which was located behind the school. My heart was pounding as I saw him jog across the football field to meet me. We introduced ourselves to each other and made plans for him to visit me. He came to visit me several times and we became friends. I let him know how I wished it could have been more, but nothing changed. He promised me that we would always be friends. I enjoyed our time together while it lasted. He ended up marrying a girl he met when he was away visiting his grandmother in another city. When he told me about it my heart was torn to pieces.

My first job was working at an amusement park as a park attendant during the summer of 1981. I had lots of fun working there. Sometimes after work the manager would let all the workers ride the rides for thirty minutes. We usually were able to ride at least 4 or 5 different rides in that time. After the summer ended and I was back in school, the Co-op class gave me the opportunity to work at the city library in my senior year of high school. This is when I came to believe that I would write a book one day. I loved being in the library, there were so many books, so many stories, and I read a new book every week. Then I met Hanslee during the summer of 1983 and I believed that I would live happily ever after. I graduated from high school the following year in May of 1984, and I was finally happy again. I wanted to go to college but my mother said she couldn't afford it. So when I was old enough I applied for a student loan, which allowed me to go to college. I went to several business colleges and then I realized that I wanted to pursue a bachelor's degree in accounting, which I began working on in 1999, when I moved to the Kansas City area.

My History

My memory of Granddaddy Dan, my maternal grandfather, is very simple. I can remember my mother taking my siblings and me to visit him quite often, maybe two or three times a week. He lived with a very nice lady who welcomed us as if she was our grandmother. My grandfather was a very kind fellow. He died at the age of 83 of cancer. There was such a sense of loss that my children would never experience the love I had experienced with this wonderful man.

My memory of Mama Mary, my maternal grandmother, is very rich with wonderful events. She took care of my sister, my brother and me because my mother was practically a child herself. I remember how Mama Mary would cook red beans, rice and brown gravy, homemade cornbread, and fried chicken almost every day. On Sundays she cooked extras—like sweet potatoes, homemade macaroni and cheese, and mustard greens. I felt like I was in heaven. I'll never forget the taste of her homemade biscuits she cooked for us every Saturday and Sunday morning. I loved combing her hair as she sat on the front porch in her old rocking chair almost every day before the sun went down. It was so wonderful growing up in her house.

As a child I was always taken to church (Baptist Church), thanks to Mama Mary. I learned many Bible stories, including the story of Joseph and the coat of many colors, the three men in the fiery furnace, and many more. I can remember one particular sermon that stands out in my mind—Christians should not have sex before marriage. After that sermon, I developed a strong desire to understand God's Word for myself, so I began to read the Holy Bible and learned that what the preacher said was true. Even though I believed God's Word was true, after becoming a teenager, I still took the wrong path. I loved God and wanted to please him, but I allowed my emotions to rule my heart, and so I did the very thing God says not to do. However, I continued to read His Word and I realized God was still the only way out of any dilemma I found myself in.

I was 22 when my grandmother got sick. I was terrified of losing her. I prayed and God gave me the strength to accept her passing in February of 1988.

My memory of Clifton Richardson, Jr., my father, is very vague. I don't remember my father holding me when I was a young child. Somehow I just *"knew"* when he came to visit that he was my father. I dreaded seeing him leave. "I'll be back soon," he said. But soon to me was a long time. He came to visit me four or five times in all my forty-four years. I had always wanted to develop a personal relationship with my father, but he died in May of 2006 before we could form a father-daughter relationship. That really tore me apart inside. Even though I did not have the opportunity to have a personal relationship with my father, I am glad to know he accepted Jesus Christ as his

Savior before he passed away. This taught me that having a relationship with Jesus is what makes the difference. Now I know I will have a relationship with my father in heaven.

I asked my mother to tell me about my history and when she did, I was shocked. My mother told me about my maternal grandmother, my maternal grandfather, her relationship with my father, and about a memorable person from her past.

My mother, Ethel Dunn, was 11 years old when her parents separated. My grandmother was abusive to my grandfather. Later my grandmother met a man who became abusive to her. The man attempted to cut her head off, but my grandmother fought back and stabbed him with an ice pick. The ambulance arrived and took him to the hospital. The police took my grandmother to jail. My mother also remembers my grandmother serving time in jail for the stabbing. She's not sure how long. She and my Uncle Charles had to live with my eldest aunt, Essie, until my grandmother was released from jail. My mother couldn't understand why my grandmother had to spend time in jail for protecting herself from a man who tried to kill her.

My mother met my dad at one of her friend's house. He took an interest in her and they began dating. In 1966 I was born out of wedlock and my father was not present for the delivery. I asked Mother if she knew why he wasn't there. She replied, "No, I don't know why."

When I was four years old my father left Louisiana and moved to Seattle, Washington. Six months later, he returned to Louisiana and told my mother he was engaged to be married. She found out later he had lied and was *already* married. I can remember asking my mother many times as a young girl, "Where's my daddy? When will he be coming to visit?" She would always tell me he was away in Seattle and she did not know when he would return.

When I was 9, my mother was in an abusive relationship that lasted 20 years. She finally realized she wanted something better. After Mama Mary told my mother she needed to start taking care of her own children, she realized some things had to change to make a better life for us. She decided to leave the abusive relationship, stop drinking and smoking (cold turkey) and she began taking care of us like a mother should. She became a wonderful mother.

I later became aware of the generational pattern of abuse in my family. Even though it is known that boys raised in an abusive home are more likely to become batterers, I pray the generational pattern stops with me, and my three boys will not become batterers or victims of domestic violence.

Don't Die for Love

In the following pages you'll read how I entered Zunta House, a place for battered women. *Some women, who love their abuser so much, never make it to a place like the Zunta House because their abuser kills them before they decide to call for help.* The love they have for their abuser cannot stop the abuser from taking their life.

When I first went to Zunta House I saw a sign that read "Don't Die for Love." I had been thinking of a title for my life story ever since Hanslee and I met. I thought my story would be a romance, but time proved me wrong. The words in the sign stuck with me but I did not know why until April 26, 2001. I received a phone call from my sister and it became clear. I will never be able to say it enough—"God was watching over me." Those words came alive in my life after that phone call. I hope my story will touch others in a special way, even if it is just one person. I hope my story will cause others to think about love in a different way. If love hurts, get out immediately—life is too short. The Holy Bible says, "Life is but a vapor."

Mary Barton is my maternal aunt. She was a big encouragement in my life, before she passed away. I include the poem she wrote in loving memory of her.

Life's Disappointments

In life there's disappointments
But don't let them bother you
If you believe what God has
Said He'll surely see you through
Life is filled with sorrow
Our hearts are filled with pain
Sometimes we ask for sunshine
And then He gives us rain
He said He knows our hearts
And this I know is true
He has stood beside me
And He will do the same for you
Disappointment is no friend of mine
But don't let it block your way
Just put your trust in God
And live from day to day
But when your burdens get heavy
And trouble gets in your way
Just say I thank you Lord for
Teaching me how to pray

Mary Barton, 1939 – 2000

Love at First Sight

One beautiful day in April of 1983, it was as if summer had arrived early. I was 17, soon to be a senior in high school, and I was living in Baton Rouge, Louisiana, the place known for its humid subtropical climate, thunderstorms during the summer and constant threat of hurricanes and tornadoes. I was standing on my porch enjoying the sun and the cool breeze when I saw a young guy walking toward our house. He walked as if he had confidence and knew where he was headed.

"Hello!" the young guy said.

He's captivating, I thought, as he got closer. The manly fragrance he wore was breath-taking. He looked to be about five-seven and to weigh about 168 pounds. He was neatly dressed in a polo shirt and blue jeans and I was very impressed to see that he had a belt on and his shirt tucked in. He had nice coal-black curly hair, perfectly shaped eyes, nose, cheeks and lips, with a light chocolate color complexion. It's love, I thought to myself. He's the man for me.

"Is your roof in need of repairs?" He asked.   His voice was very sexy and masculine, I thought as he spoke to me.

"Wait," I said. I ran inside the house. "Mother, there's a guy outside asking if you want your roof repaired!"

"He'll need to ask our landlord," my mother answered. I went back outside and relayed the message.

"What's your name?" the young guy asked, staring into my eyes.

"Darlene," I replied. I felt the blood in my cheeks become warm and the palms of my hands began to sweat.

"I'm Hanslee, but everyone calls me Lee. Can I call you?" he asked.

"I guess," I replied. I ran into the house, wrote my number down on a piece of paper and I thought about how amazing it felt to finally be noticed. In high school the guys passed me up. I ran back outside and gave him the piece of paper.

"I'll call you tonight," Hanslee said. My heart was pounding as I watched him walk away.

After he left, I couldn't stop thinking about him. I anxiously anticipated his call that night. It seemed like the phone took forever to ring. I sat on the couch in the living room, watching the phone on the end table beside me. My mother, Ethel, was in her room. My sister, Loretta, wasn't there because she had her own place, and my brother, Keith, was in his room. My mother didn't mind me talking on the phone. It was like she had confidence in my sister and my brother and me to make the right decisions. I guess it was because my grandmother raised us. The phone finally rang, and with butterflies in my stomach I picked up the receiver.

"Hello!" I said.

"May I speak to Darlene?" Hanslee asked.

"This is she," I said.

"Can I come see you?" Hanslee asked. "I'm not good at talking on the phone."

I was ecstatic that he wanted to see me again so soon. He came over that night and we talked for a long time. Before he left, he kissed me softly on my lips and it felt like love. I had butterflies in my stomach all evening.

I remember that for a while after we met, all we did was sit on the couch at my house getting better acquainted. Every time he came over he had a quart of beer and/ or a pint of wine. He never asked me out on a date, like to the movies or dinner, and not even to his house, which was okay with me. All I cared about was being together. He told me all about his family and I told him all about mine.

He told me about his mother and father and about his life with them. He said he had twelve siblings. While growing up he remembered seeing a new baby each year for about eight years straight. When each child turned nine months old, he and his older sisters had to help take care of them. He and his siblings were never allowed in his mother's room, but he never told me the reason why. He said he ran away from home when he was fourteen, because he thought it would be easier on his mother and father. He realized later that this hurt them more than it helped.

His father was a hard-working man, working two and sometimes three jobs at a time. Hanslee and his brothers would have to go with his father to work to help out. Most of the time, his father was very tired, which meant Hanslee and his brothers had to complete most of the cleaning work while their father slept in one of the office chairs. This caused Hanslee to struggle academically in school. He spoke highly of his father. He wished he could be the man his father was.

At the end of that summer in July, I helped Hanslee move into a new place. The place was a furnished little efficiency, two rooms with a bedroom kitchen combination and a bathroom. The furnisher that was in the place was an old style queen size bed, dresser and chair. He needed things like a fan, pots, plates, utensils, towels, sheets, blanket, and soap. He and I piled all those things into my car, an old black 1978 Oldsmobile, and I drove him to his new place. After we put everything away, we sat down on the bed and

Hanslee gave me a hug and a kiss. "Thank you for helping me tonight," he said as he held me in his arms.

I stayed and we talked for a couple of hours. I told him about my younger days. About the time we lived with my grandmother until I was a teenager and that my mother worked as Nanny for a white lady during the day and she work at a night club at night. We didn't see my mother much, because of her two jobs. We only saw her when she was asleep, leaving for work or on Saturday and Sunday mornings. My sister, my brother, and I cried every time she left home because we wanted to go with her. One time I hid in the back of my mother's station wagon, so that I could go to work with her and I ended up having a lot of fun that day with my mother, even though she fussed at me for doing that. I told him about my sister, that she was very smart but she would not help me be smart like her. I felt that everybody, especially my grandmother loved Loretta more than me. And about my bother Keith, that he was very mean to me when my mother was away.

Then he made passionate love to me. Every other night after that, I stayed over at his place. He became the apple of my eye and I fell deeper in love with him. I lost something that I could never get back, my virginity. I never thought I would live to regret it, because it felt like love when it happened. Since I had given myself to him, I thought he would ask me to marry him. Then I asked him if he would ever ask me to be his wife. "We are already married," he exclaimed. "Promise me that I'll be the only one," he continued. I believe him so I promised.

In 1984, I was a senior at Capital Senior High School. Hanslee and I had been going together for about seven months and school was almost over. One day while at school in the cafeteria during lunch, my friend Sandra asked, "Who are you dating, Darlene?"

"Hanslee," I replied.

Carla, another friend of mine said, "There is this girl named Keisha who goes to school here and I don't know if you know but she told me her boyfriend's name is Lee. I wonder if that's the same guy, Darlene. Maybe you should ask him about it. He might be seeing both of you at the same time," she chuckled.

I was shocked to hear that anyone else knew him, but then again, he had told me everyone called him Lee. Hanslee told me he had just move to Baton Rouge six months prior to meeting me. Before he moved into his new place, he said he rented a room from a guy named Wally. I just figured he couldn't be the same person Carla was talking about. I couldn't wait to see Hanslee again; I wanted to tell him what I had heard at school.

Later that day, Hanslee came over to my house and we sat in the living room. He sat on one end of the sofa and I sat on the other end. He was looking straight ahead. With my feet tucked under me, I pressed my hands together, then slowly folded my arms and asked, "Do you know a girl name Keisha? Is she your girlfriend?"

"No, I don't have a girlfriend," he replied. I scooted closer to him. He was so sincere and calm; I believed him and dropped the subject.

A few weeks later, I was hanging out with my cousin, Joy, at her house. After we fried some chicken and ate, we decided to pay Hanslee a visit.

When we arrived at his house, his ten-speed-bike was parked in the usual spot, on the side of the house. I knocked on the door but he did not answer. I went around to the back to knock on the window. It was dark so I couldn't see anything, but I heard the fan. "Hanslee," I called. He still didn't answer. I went back to the front.

"His bike is right there and that means he's home," I said to Joy.

I knocked for five more minutes, and then we left. My heart was pounding with anger. I felt betrayed. I desperately wanted to know how he could do this to me. He said he loved me; he said I was his wife. He said he didn't know her. Those thoughts paced through my mind and it was difficult for me to sleep that night.

When I arrived at school the next day, I checked the absentee list and Keisha's name was listed. I could hardly wait until the last bell rang.

While I was riding the bus home, I played back his exact words in my mind. "No, I don't have a girlfriend." I'm so stupid, I whispered to myself. Why didn't I ask more questions? I'm going over there right now, I told myself. He's got to tell me I'm the only one. My stomach felt shaky and I couldn't stop the tears from falling down my face. I had trouble sitting back in my seat on the bus. Her name was on the absentee list and he did not come to the door last night. I was not convinced those things happened as a coincidence.

Finally, I arrived at his house and knocked on the door. His bike hadn't been moved since I saw it the night before.

"Hanslee, I know you're in there," I called as my voice shivered. "Why aren't you opening the door?"

"Go home, Darlene, I'm coming over to your house later," he yelled from the other side of the door.

I felt stupid standing there, but I was not leaving. After about ten minutes he opened the door a crack, which allowed me to furiously push the door all the way open. I saw Keisha in his bed, covered with a sheet but she was undressed. I noticed the kitchen knife I had loaned to him, lying on the counter. I grabbed that knife and charged at him. He grabbed my wrist and I shoved against him. He twisted my arm back and wrenched the knife away from me. All I could do was cry. Keisha did not move or say a word.

"Get up and put on some clothes," he commanded her.

As she walked to the restroom covered with my blanket, I said, "You better not breathe a word of this to anybody at school, because if you do, I will beat your..., so help me... (I swore at her)." She looked at me as if she was horrified of what I would do to her, but she didn't say a word.

I walked outside, sat on the steps of Hanslee's house and continued to cry. Hanslee came and sat down beside me. "I'm sorry," he said. "I'll come see you later."

"Don't even bother. Just bring me my stuff," I said sadly and walked away. I was angry and wounded all at the same time.

I went home. Every night for several months, I cried and prayed he would come back to see me, even if it was just to be friends.

Then I saw Keisha waiting for the city bus six months later. She was pregnant. My heart broke into a million pieces for the second time, because he had chosen her over me.

I didn't see Hanslee again until the spring of 1986. He had gotten himself a car by then and he drove by every once in a while. He'd call me over to the car and say, "Hi, Sweets. How are you?"

"I'm okay," I replied. I loved it when he called me that.

One evening he actually parked his car and came in. "Would you like something to eat?" I asked him, after we joined my mother and brother in the dining room watching television.

"No thanks," he replied.

"Can I get you something to eat?" I asked again after my mother and brother left the room.

"Yeah, I guess." He seemed ashamed and acted like he was in some kind of trouble with my family and me. Maybe he thought we didn't like him anymore, but it wasn't that way. I did not mind being there for him as a friend and wanted to show him I cared very much for him.

Every time he came by, I noticed a baby seat in the back of his car, which suggested that Keisha was carrying his baby the day I saw her. The beer and wine containers suggested he was still a heavy drinker. He told me he started drinking when he was just twelve years old. When we were together I constantly encouraged him to stop drinking but it seemed like the encouragement did no good. So I figured I'd simply continue to pray for him to change. After a few casual visits, he stopped coming by.

During the fall of 1986 I met a guy name Stephen at church. I admired him a lot because he was so handsome and charming. I desperately tried to convince him that I was the one for him, but he admired my sister, Loretta. She was much prettier than me. Her skin complexion was lighter than mine. She was thinner than me. She always had pretty long hair, unlike me; I always had short stubby hair. Everyone in my family called me "Baldy Blue," and I hated being called that. Most everyone thought I was older than my sister.

Stephen later told Loretta to tell me that his brother PJ wanted to meet me. We met but Stephen failed to tell me PJ had a wife and three children. PJ told me that he was in the process of filing for a divorce even though he still loved his three girls.

"I think we should wait until your divorce is final and then see each other," I pointed out to PJ.

"But I love you and nobody else, not even my wife. It's over between us. I want to take care of you. You're beautiful." PJ exclaimed. I was vulnerable, spiritually blinded by my feelings to the truth, and I was just a kid. So after he told me everything I thought I wanted to hear, I agreed to start seeing him anyway. We decided, though, to wait until his divorce was final before we became intimate.

One night I was at my sister's house and PJ called. "Can I come over?" he asked. He came and we watched television for a while. Then we started to cuddle and the decision to wait changed and it happened. After that night we had fun. We went to the movies and out to dinner a couple of times. I had begun to believe that even though I was still in love with Hanslee, somehow PJ would help me to forget about him. PJ promised to marry me after he got a divorce and I looked forward to it.

Two months had passed and ironically PJ stopped calling me or coming over. I called him several times at his mother's house, where he said he was staying. He was never there. I pondered about what was going on with him, so I continued to call. Then, a month later, I went to doctor and she said, "Darlene you're pregnant." I couldn't believe it. My life is over, I thought. I wanted PJ to know, so I called his mother and asked her to tell him the news. She informed me that she had not heard from or seen PJ in a while. She figured he was back with his wife.

After talking to her, I cried every night for three weeks because he had lied to me. I thought he loved me. I thought I was beautiful to him. I thought I was the one he wanted to take care of. Thinking about all that stuff—the lies—made me hurt deep down in my soul. I gave myself to him and I trusted him with my heart. I wanted to know if his mother told him I was pregnant, so I kept trying to contact him. Then a couple of months later I talked to PJ on the phone.

"I'm pregnant," I informed him.

"This is not a good time to have a baby," he replied. "I'll give you some money to go to the doctor," he continued to say, implying that he wanted me to have an abortion.

"You can go to hell and burn," I said and hung up the phone.

Eleven months after I had met PJ, around July of 1987, Hanslee appeared again. I heard a knock at the door and

I ran to see who it was. I was still living with my mother. When I saw him, I was the happiest person in the world. I walked out onto the porch to talk to him, the cool breeze tickling my bare feet. I wanted to hug him, but I didn't because I was eight months pregnant and I didn't know what he would say.

"Look at you, Missy!" he said as if he was surprised by what he saw.

"Where have you been?" I asked.

"Florida," he replied in a very upbeat way. "I see you've been busy."

It was like we were meeting for the very first time and starting a new relationship with the past behind us. I felt the butterflies, flushed cheeks and sweaty palms again. He came back the next night and we sat in his car and kept each other company. He told me more stories about what he did in Florida. He told me about how he had tried some PCP and the affects it had on him. He made me laugh so hard that I almost wet my pants. Then I told him all about PJ, my baby's father, how I had to tell PJ to go to hell. I was very surprised and happy that Hanslee came back the next night.

The Abuse Starts

In December 1988, I finally received a public housing certificate, which gave me the opportunity to get my own apartment. I applied for a certificate because I couldn't afford to pay rent with the salary I was making and I did not want to live with my mother any longer, since I had become a mother myself.

I moved to Scotlandville, a little town in Louisiana about eight miles from my mother's house. My son Bradrell, who was then sixteen months, and I didn't have much, but that was okay because we had each other. I loved my little one-bedroom apartment. It had a living room, a kitchen-dining room combination, one bathroom, and one bedroom big enough for my bed and Bradrell's yellow-framed baby bed.

We had to use a cooler until God provided us with a nice used refrigerator about two months later. My mother gave me a table and I found a lot of nice things at garage sales and thrift shops around town. It turned out to be a nice home I could call my own.

Hanslee continued to come by to see me when I got my new place. He claimed he would get a real job and stop hustling, if I let him come live with me. I agreed, but it wasn't long before he started staying out late, night after night.

One Friday night after I had picked Hanslee up from work he wanted to go somewhere. "Let me use your car?" he asked.

"No," I replied.

"Okay, drop me off somewhere then," he said. He didn't care that Bradrell was sleeping. I covered Bradrell up with his baby blanket and laid him on the back seat of the car, hoping he wouldn't wake up, and took Hanslee where he wanted to go, to avoid arguing with him. When we arrived, it was an old closed down building. "I need you to come back in two hours," he commanded.

"Okay," I agreed. I felt knots in my stomach, because I was very concerned about what he was up to. I bit my lip softly to keep from asking him to tell me what he was planning to do. I went back home and watched the clock for two hours. Then I covered Bradrell up again with his baby blanket, put him on the back seat, and drove back to the old building.

"Pop the trunk, hurry!" Hanslee said in a shaky tone.

I popped the trunk and laid my head on arm against the steering wheel in despair. What is he doing? I wondered.

What have I gotten myself into? He came around to the passenger's side of the car and tapped on the window.

When I unlocked the door, he got in and said, "Let's go!" He was breathing very rapidly. "Go to your mother's house." I drove to my mother's house, still wondering what he was up to.

"Park in the back," he said. It was about 12:00 a.m. when we got there. I parked in the back of my mother's house on the carport, which was in the back yard. I got Bradrell and his bag out of the car and went into the house. My mother was asleep, so I turned on the television with the volume down to make sure not to wake her, and sat down on the sofa in the family room. I laid my son on the sofa beside me. I watched TV for about twenty minutes and then I went back outside to see what Hanslee was doing. I saw him standing about seven feet away from a fire he had made. The flames were almost ten feet high.

"What are you doing?" I shrieked. "I hope my mother doesn't come out here." He was burning the black rubber off the copper wires he had taken from the abandoned building.

"Don't worry, she won't. I know what I'm doing. This is going to make us a lot of money," he explained confidently.

I went back into the house. I could hardly focus on the TV because I couldn't stop thinking about what I had gotten myself into. After about an hour, he came in the house. His hands and clothes were covered in soot. He went to the restroom to wash his hands and then we left.

We drove back home. He took his clothes off, got his beer and wine out of the refrigerator and started bragging about how much more money he made in one night hustling electric wire from old buildings than he would make working an honest job. I put Bradrell in his bed, changed into something comfortable and joined him in the living room. I listened intently as he explained how he pulled it off. He finally shut up and made love to me, which seemed to be the best part of our relationship. I had started working for Stanacola Medical Clinic in September of that same year. I was so worn out that night and I was relieved because I didn't work Saturdays and wouldn't have to call in sick. Later that morning he wanted to sell the wire.

"Take me to Southern Scraps," he commanded. It was a business that sold reusable metal, iron and copper. I took him.

He promised to give me some of the money, and he did, but a few days later he demanded I give it back to him, because he spent all of his part of the money. After helping him with his hustles several more times, I stopped, because what he was doing was wrong and my conscience would not allow me to continue helping him with his shady deals.

"You said you would get an honest job," I reminded him. He complained about making pennies when he worked an honest job. Finally, I told him I was not going to take him to pull wires anymore. He didn't like that.

One night he invited one of his buddies to the apartment. He said, "This is my friend Anthony and he's going to stay with us tonight. He's going to help me with my hustle since you won't."

I walked to my room and he followed me. "He can't stay here," I said. "Have you forgotten I live in public housing?" He did not like me telling him how I felt. He closed the door and slapped me in the face several times. He hit me so hard it felt like my brain shifted in my head and I could hear my neck pop a few times. I tried to cover my face, but he moved my hand each time. I cried and pleaded with him to stop.

He finally did, but as he left the room he said, "Don't you ever embarrass me in front of my friend."

I held my face and cried, lying on my bed. My face and ears were throbbing with intense pain, and I felt humiliated. Then I went to check on Bradrell; he was in his walker in the living room. Hanslee had walked outside to talk to his friend.

I need to leave, I thought. I'm not staying another minute. I grabbed my son and his baby bag and headed for the door. Hanslee was coming in at the same time.

"Where are you going?" he asked.

"I can't stay here," I answered.

"You don't need to go anywhere. Sit down. I'm sorry." He walked in front of me, face to face, body to body, and feet to feet causing me to walk backward and forcing me to sit on the sofa. I still had Bradrell in my arms. "I'm not going to do anything to you," he assured me.

He gently took Bradrell from me and put him in his baby bed. I ran out the door and got into my car. I wanted to go to my mother's house, but I thought about my baby. I couldn't leave him. And I was mad. That was my house, and if anyone should leave, it ought to be Hanslee. I looked up at the window of my apartment, located on the second floor of the apartment building, several times and saw him peeking out. After sitting there for about forty minutes, I went back upstairs to my apartment and found Bradrell asleep in his bed and Hanslee sitting on the sofa watching TV.

"You're back, I see, Sweets," he said. "Where you been?"

"Sitting in my car," I replied. Then I took a bath and went to bed.

After that night, he said he was sorry but continued staying out late. Several times I noticed him coming out of the next door neighbor's apartment, which made me very angry. I talked to him about it and he wanted me to believe he was hanging out with the girl's brother.

By the Spring of 1989 I was fed up with him staying out late and going into that woman's house next door. I wanted to know what was really going on. So one night when he was hanging out over there, I put Bradrell in his baby bed and went over and knocked on the door. The woman opened the door. "Is Lee here?" I asked.

"Yes, come on in," she replied. I could see him as he walked back to the bathroom. I followed behind him to ask him what was going on and when he was coming home. He was talking like he had something in his mouth.

"What's wrong with you?" I asked.

"Nothing," he replied. "Let's go home."

I walked out and he came behind me. I checked on my baby, saw that he was sleeping and went back into the living room and joined Hanslee on the sofa for a while. He seemed like he'd had too much to drink or was on some type of drug. He talked to me as if he hadn't done anything wrong. After about twenty minutes, he left. When I walked outside to see where he was, he was walking away from the apartment and then disappeared into the night. I walked back into my apartment and wondered where he could have gone. I should have been glad he walked out of my life again, but I was sad things hadn't worked out for us.

I loved him with all my being, but I realized later it was best that he was gone. After several nights of weeping, I began to accept the fact that it was the best thing for me. Unfortunately, two months after we broke up, I learned I was pregnant with Hanslee's child. I was very hurt that I had to endure another pregnancy alone. Hanslee III was born in December of 1989. While Hanslee was away I attended church on a regular basis and I concentrated on taking care of my two beautiful children; they were a blessing from the Lord. I must admit there were many times I wished that Hanslee would come back around even if it was just to form a relationship with his son. I found out later that he was living with Keisha and she had another child by him, who was born in September of 1990. Nine months after Hanslee III was born I went back to work.

I'll Never Go Back - I Love Him,
I Must Go Back

In April 1991, when Hanslee III was almost two years old, I allowed his father back into my life. I had already forgiven him for the past and I really wanted to be with him. I also wanted Hanslee III to know his father. For a couple of weeks, Hanslee looked for a job and made an effort to be respectful to me. He called his mother and dad so I could talk with them. His mother told me all about the way Hanslee's father treated her. I was appalled by what she told me. She said his father beat her when she was six months pregnant. She told me about how the Lord delivered her from alcoholism and after that she became a preacher. She prayed Hanslee would not hurt me. She said, "Lord, if Hanslee is not there to help Darlene, then move him out of her life."

After awhile Hanslee started drinking, doing drugs with the neighbors next door again, and belittling and verbally abusing me. I was extremely stressed and unable to rest the night before I had to go to work.

By June of that same year, I found myself watching every move Hanslee made; it really wore me down mentally, so I ended up quitting my job. I just couldn't do it anymore. I prayed for a miracle. I was too afraid to break up with him because he was too selfish to leave and allow the boys and me to stay in my apartment without harassing us. My mother, sister, and brother were my miracle. They helped me move all my belongings out of the apartment while he was away. I'm not sure where Hanslee ended up after that. I promised myself I would never tell him where I lived, but deep down I still hoped we could be friends so Hanslee III could have a relationship with his father.

Three months after I moved into my new place on Melon Court, Hanslee called me at my mother's house, while I was visiting. He wanted me to believe that he was a different person by making the same old promises, saying that he wouldn't stay out late or hit me again. He asked if he could come see me.

"I'm so sorry," he said. Hearing from him brought comfort to my heart. I missed him so much and felt he was sincere, so I agreed. I enjoyed spending time with him at my mother's. Taking my hands and looking straight into my eyes, he promised, "Things will be different." The attention he gave me made me realize how lonely I was, and that my love for him was as strong as ever. I wanted to trust him, so I did, a little.

That October I was attending school at Delta College of Technology. In class one morning I found myself thinking about my relationship with Hanslee. He was staying with a friend and he complained about it. Every time he came to visit me at my mother's house he would ask me if he could come see me at my house instead of at my mother's.

"When can I come to your house?" he inquired.

"Soon," I answered. I was afraid to fully trust him again and I didn't know what else to say. My mind was so confused with whether I should let him come to visit me at my house because I knew the next question would be, "When can I move back in?" He was at my mother's house waiting for me after I got out of school. He was sitting on the sofa in the living room.

I sat down beside him and looked him straight in the eyes, "Will you promise not to go hustling anymore?" I pleaded.

"I need some money. How can I promise you that?" he argued.

I didn't know what else to say, so I left and went to the Martin Luther King Community Center to do some community service. I thought more about what he had said. I guess he had to make money somehow, I thought. I love him. I miss him and I need him to love me. My heart wouldn't let me say no.

That night he came to visit me at my house and two days later I made it official. I told him it was okay for him to move back in. In my heart I yearned, yet again, for things to change. A couple of weeks later guilt began to set in, even though things were better.

When we made love, I regretted it because we weren't married. I wanted what other people had: a family and happiness. At the same time, I wanted to live a Christian life. I had a choice to make. I tried to talk it over with Hanslee but he didn't want to deal with it. Then one night we were sitting in the living room watching TV when I said, "Hanslee, if you're not planning to marry me and straighten up your life by getting a real job, we should go our separate ways."

"We don't need any papers to say we are married. We're married in our hearts. And I have a job," he replied.

Happiness, I tried to convince him, came only through having a relationship with Jesus, but he didn't want to hear that. I wanted so much for us to be a family, God's way. I shared my feelings about how much I would love to have a relationship with his other two children, Jay and Jason. I called Keisha and asked her how she felt about letting our children meet each other. She suggested it was Hanslee's responsibility to make arrangements for that. I told him what she had said, but he did nothing about it.

I began to wonder if he really loved me because it seemed he found something wrong with everything I wanted to do. At Christmas time, I asked him for some money to buy toys for our children.

"I gave you some money and you didn't get any toys?" he said. He expected me to pay bills and buy toys with a hundred and twenty dollars. He made me feel so bad about everything I did.

"How could I? I paid the light bill and bought food for us to eat. All I want to do is give my kids a nice Christmas, but all you think about is supporting your habit—smoking, drinking and doing drugs!" I exclaimed.

"We lead two different lives, Darlene," he complained.

"Leave, then," I insisted.

"You just want to run my life," he said.

"You just don't understand me," I replied. But I knew he was not listening, so I left and went to my mother's house.

Over and over again I asked myself, why am I still with him? I hated the verbal abuse. I had not misused his money. I had used my own money to buy a baby doll for his daughter Jay, a truck for Bradrell, and building blocks for Hanslee III and Jason. Hanslee complained about my cooking and about how I took care of the children. One minute he wanted to fight and the next minute he wanted to make love. I didn't understand, and continually wondered why things couldn't be right with us.

When Hanslee made love to me, it brought tears to my eyes. I longed to know how he could bring both tears of joy and tears of sorrow to my eyes. One minute I was happy just being with him, never wanting to leave, and the next minute I longed to be far away and never see him again.

When we were together, the bad outweighed the good; the cruelty was unbearable at times. But when we were apart he wanted to know where I had been and what took me so long to return. I didn't want to go home that night but I went anyway because I was tired of being at my mother's house.

Hanslee Moves to Clovis, New Mexico

By July 1992, Hanslee's drinking had gone into overdrive. When he gave me money, he accused me of spending it on myself, which I never did, but he made me feel so bad about myself. The physical abuse began again in August of that same year. The boys were asleep in their room and I had already gone to bed one night when he came home late. He climbed into bed without taking a bath, smelling of vomit and alcohol. I couldn't stand the smell, so I got up and went into the living room to watch TV. He followed me and continued to agitate me.

"What's wrong?" Hanslee asked.

"Nothing!" I shrieked.

He came to the couch where I was sitting, sat on me and leaned his body on my head and neck. I didn't say anything at first, so he leaned harder, as if trying to force me to speak. It felt as if my neck would break, and after about five minutes I couldn't keep silent any longer.

"Stop it!" I demanded. "You're hurting me!" I said as I pushed him off of me and walked to the kitchen.

He followed me and then grabbed both my arms just below my armpits. I tried to pull away from him, but he picked me up and threw me to the floor. My hipbone felt like it had cracked.

"See what you made me do!" he yelled as he walked back into the living room.

I sat there shaking, my legs folded in my arms and my head on my knees, crying. I thanked God for protecting me that night. I did not have the energy to leave; my hip was still hurting so I continued sitting there for a while.

Finally Hanslee came back into the kitchen and said, "I'm sorry. Can you please forgive me?" He would not leave me alone until I accepted his weak apology. He helped me up and led me to the bed, where I quietly cried myself to sleep. But not before I came up with a plan.

The next morning I rose with my mind made up. I was not going to live that way any longer. I woke Hanslee at the usual time for work. As he was leaving, I said, "I will not be here when you come home."

"Why?" he asked.

"You know the answer to that question," I replied.

My words stopped him in his tracks. He went outside and told the guy who came to pick him up for work that he wasn't going. Then he came back into the house and went back to sleep, as if that would stop me from leaving. I got my kids and went to my mother's house for a few days.

My cousin, Gretia, convinced me to call the police to make him get out of my house. "That's your house," she said. "You shouldn't have to leave."

The police went to my house to tell Hanslee he had to leave, but he wasn't there. They came back to my mother's house to report that they hadn't seen him. I assumed he was hiding in the house somewhere, so I didn't go back home right away.

A week later, he had the nerve to show up at my mother's house.

"Sweets, when are you coming home?" he wanted to know.

"Our relationship is over," I told him, tears rolling down my cheeks. "Things are not working out for us. We want different things. You want to drink and spend your time far away in your own little made-up world. I want to live a peaceful life with Jesus as my savior. I want to get married, but you say that's stupid."

"Darlene, if I get on that bus to Clovis, New Mexico, I'm never looking back," he warned.

Several weeks prior to this incident, when Hanslee had almost broken my neck, his father had called and offered him a job. We weren't getting along, and he didn't like working in Baton Rouge. I advised him to take the job with his dad. His father sent him a bus ticket to Clovis.

I let him get on that bus, praying that if he came back it would be as a changed man. I hated to see him leave. I could not stop wondering if he was truly sorry that day.

With Hanslee gone, I often thought about how different our lives were. His life consisted of late nights, marijuana, beer and wine. My life consisted of going to church and working on changing for the better. Thinking about these things helped me realize it was best that we were apart.

During our separation, I longed for him to hold me in his arms and tell me he loved me as much as I loved him. I called him several times and he'd call me once in a while. When I talked to him, he would complain about how his mother was treating him while he was in Clovis. He also talked about how his mother had treated him when he was younger. He said his mother was the reason he and his brother and sisters received whippings. Every time they disobeyed their mother, she would report it to their father and he would discipline them. He blamed his mother for all their family problems in the past. He said a lot of bad things about her. I never could understand how he could talk so poorly of his own mother. I always tried to say something to make him forget about the past and focus on the future, but nothing I said seem to make any difference. Everybody who knew Hanslee had doubts that he would ever change, but I believed God could help him. I asked the Lord to save Hanslee and send him back because I really missed him.

Prayer and attending church was very much a part of my life while Hanslee was away. Our separation really affected me badly. I could not stop thinking about him and hoping that he would allow God to save him. I found comfort during our separation in journaling, which allowed me to release my pent-up thoughts, awaken my inner voice and soothe my troubled memories. I remember there were many times I wanted to tell Hanslee something but was afraid to, so I would write it in my journal.

In September 1994, I wrote in my journal about a church service I attended one Sunday that truly strengthened my faith in God and helped me stop focusing on my separation from Hanslee. The preacher said, "We should be glad God woke us up this morning. We should be glad that we are in the house of the Lord. There is no one like the Father, the Son, and the Holy Ghost. Amen, Amen. The Father sent His Son, Jesus to save sinners. We should be thankful and accept the gift of salvation. The Son Jesus sent the Holy Spirit to be our comforter to help relieve our grief and anxieties. We should be thankful. When you seek a relationship with Jesus, you learn to obey him and live morally. Jesus said, 'Take up your cross and follow me. Learn of me for my yoke is easy.' As Sister Loretta sings, for those of you who feel led to accept Jesus today as your personal Savior, come to the altar." As he preached, I sat there thinking about how I wished Hanslee was sitting beside me hearing the wonderful words of God concerning salvation, then our relationship would be so much better. I thought if he accepted Christ as his personal savior, it would make him think twice before hitting me. There were several people who went to the altar as Loretta sang, "God Specializes in Things Thought Impossible." The words to this song brought tears to my eyes—

Have you any rivers that you think are un-crossable?

Have you any mountains that you can't tunnel through?

God specializes in things thought impossible

And He will do what no other power can do.

Have you ever been on your bed of affliction

And the doctor says he has done all he can do?

God specializes in things thought impossible

And He will do what no other power can do.

When your body is filled with disease

And the medicine won't give you no ease,

God specializes in things thought impossible

And He will do what no other power can do.

If you're friendless and in despair, Seems like nobody cares,

God specializes in things thought impossible

And He will do what no other power, nothing but the Holy Ghost power, can do.

—I cried because my relationship with Hanslee could be related to that song. Every time Hanslee hit me it felt like everything she sang about. It hurt me to the core of my being. Yet I loved him with all of my being. The song also gave me hope that my life could change with help from Jesus. After church, I lay across my bed and searched the Holy Scriptures for confirmation to what Pastor Larry preached about. Church services like this gave me the strength to go on and not give up on life.

On March 29, 1995, I wrote in my journal about a dream I'd had, where Hanslee was with me at my mother's house. Keisha was outside asking for him. Then all of a sudden she was in the room with us. She had two rings in her hand, one for a bride and one for a groom. She gave one of the rings to Hanslee and he stared at it in amazement. Before he could explain, I put him and Keisha out of the house. But he came back in to say, "I don't want her. I want you." He went on to explain, "Darlene, I'm saved. I accepted Jesus as my savior." Then I woke up. My dream reflected what I had been asking of God, to save Hanslee and bring him back so we could get married. This dream came at a time when I struggled to put my relationship with Hanslee behind me, but the thoughts of him lingered because I loved him very dearly.

<u>Does He Even Care?</u>

Do you care about me?
Do you have respect for me?
Can you be responsible for yourself?
Are you willing to get to know me?
Love is found in all these things, but
Addictive love allows you to be hurt
By the person you're in love with.

DFD Nance, March 28, 1999

Marriage: Can it Change Both of Us?

I had hoped to be married to Hanslee by the time I was 28 years old, and to someday having a baby girl. It wasn't until I turned 29 that I was married, but I never thought it would turn out the way it did.

On Thursday, April 6, 1995, I received a phone call from Hanslee at 3:00 a.m. I had moved back to my mother's house by then and was working for Stanacola again. I reported my income to the Section-8 office and they informed me that I had to start paying rent. I freaked out because I didn't believe I could afford to pay rent on my salary. So I moved back to my mother's house.

"I'm trying to come home," he said. "The car I got from my dad has broken down and I am stranded right outside of Clovis. Do you have some money?"

"For what?" I asked.

"I need to catch the bus," he replied.

I had saved a thousand dollars by the time Hanslee called, but I struggled a little about telling him that I could purchase a ticket for him. I had also been hoping for this day to come. My love for him still flooded my heart, and I wanted to see him.

"You'll have to ask my mother if you can stay with us," I told him. He called back a few days later to ask her permission, and she gave it. She wanted me to be happy. And so I sent him the money.

It was May before Hanslee finally returned to Baton Rouge. He looked worse than I had ever seen him. He looked like he hadn't bathed in weeks, and his hair looked as if it hadn't been cut or combed for months. His father had kicked him out and he'd been living on the streets for six months, he told me later. I couldn't believe my eyes.

However, Hanslee managed, yet again, to clean himself up and act as if he was ready and willing to change for the better. After four weeks back, he got a job at a welding company. Things went well for a while, until he started asking me to be intimate with him in mother's house. At first I said no, but I was so vulnerable. It had been such a long time since he made love to me, and I still melted at his touch.

My main purpose for living with my mother was an opportunity to save money for a house, but giving in to Hanslee's advances to be intimate brought an end to that. Knowing I had been intimate with him in her house made me feel guilty, but I couldn't bring myself to tell her. Instead, I decided to use the money I saved to move into a rental house on Wynona Street. Before I moved, Hanslee and I agreed that he would continue renting a room from my mother until he was ready to marry me.

Several weeks later he began to visit me at my new place. His visits turned into sleepovers, which led to him moving in with me again. Our relationship was still unstable, though we had some good moments. Sometimes he would confide in me, admitting how messed up his life was. When he had been drinking heavily, he would cry, and I felt such compassion for him.

He shared with me that by the time he was sixteen he had been sent to a reform school for armed robbery. He had bought a gun and used it to rob a gas station back in Clovis. He said he started a fire in the back of the store to distract one of the store clerks. Then he went around to the front and robbed the other clerk. He took the money from the register and grabbed the clerk's wallet.

He showed the wallet and credit cards to his sister. They went to a liquor store and tried to use the credit cards. While his sister was in the back of the store loading up as much as she could carry, the clerk swiped the card, and then reached for the phone. Hanslee knew something was wrong and tried to get his sister's attention. She didn't see or hear him calling her, so he left before the cops arrived. His sister was taken to jail, and the police called his mother.

"Madam, we have your daughter here at the police station. We need you to come get her," an officer informed their mother.

When Hanslee's mother picked her daughter up from the police station, she asked where the credit card had come from.

"Junior gave it to me," Hanslee's sister replied. His family called him Junior.

Hanslee told his mother the credit card was his, but later in the courtroom when his mother took the stand, she said, "Junior, you know I can't lie for you." She told the court her son had stolen the credit cards during the robbery of the gas station.

When Hanslee confided stories such as this, I wondered if he had ever been shown affection as a child. Did his mother hug and kiss him? Many times Hanslee seemed distant and lacking in compassion, with no respect for me. Perhaps his irresponsible behaviors as an adult resulted from the neglect of a mother with too many children and a demanding husband. Hanslee was on an emotional roller coaster, and I allowed him to take me along with him for many years.

Once I told Hanslee I knew what his father did to his mother. "She's a liar," he said.

"How would you know?" I asked. "You weren't ever allowed in their room."

"If he did hit her, she deserved it," he replied.

"How could you say such things about your mother?" I cried. "I don't understand it."

I told him I could never feel that way about my mother, even though she left us for my grandmother to raise. My mother was hardly ever home, but I still loved her. The times I did see her, she was on her way to work or going out to work at the nightclub. But I never loved her any less.

None of this seemed to change Hanslee's feelings about his mother at all. Gradually the good times began to fade, and I found myself thinking about how my life had been before Hanslee returned.

Back in the Fall of 1994, I became interested in being a Cell Group Leader. A Cell Group Leader is a person who sponsors Bible study, prayer and fellowship meetings in their home once a month. My role as a Cell Group Leader was to be a *Humble Model* by being a true Christian, to be a *Prayer Intercessor* by praying for myself and others, to be a *Lover of God and His Word* by setting aside time to spend with God and studying His word to teach it to others, and to be an *Organizer* by maintaining prayer lists and meeting details for location, food and child helpers. Cell Group meetings were developed because the church had such a large congregation and it was very difficult for a person to form close friendly relationships. These meetings were community support groups where a small group of people who lived close to each other could meet together to study a different Holy Bible lesson that would help them cope with everyday life. We started the meeting with praise and worship to God our Lord and Savior. Then we discussed the Bible study lesson and after that we shared a pot-luck-meal. At the end of the meeting we just fellowshipped with each other and formed close relationships. This was a fun time in my life and I really enjoyed having the meetings at my house. The meetings encouraged me and got me to thinking about my life and my relationship with God. I was learning more of God's Word, and how He could help me cope with life's challenges. My faith was important to me, and I never thought I would turn away from it.

During that time I met a wonderful man named Damien at one of the cell group meetings. He was a gentleman who obviously loved the Lord. He dressed neatly, was very physically fit, and I loved the smell of his cologne. Damien started calling me at work, asking me out to lunch, and giving me a ride to church on Sundays. He even took my sons to the park to play. He was the kind of man I needed in my life, but I was blind to the facts. So blind that I missed what God really had in store for me. Time and time again I allowed my love for Hanslee to deprive me of what I really deserved.

Now that Hanslee was back in the picture, I no longer held cell group meetings in my home. Damien was not allowed to take my kids to the park because Hanslee was jealous. Hanslee demanded that I tell Damien not to come pick up the kids anymore.

Going to the cell group meetings week after week gave me the desire to change. I was feeling guilty about being intimate with Hanslee. It was time to remind him of the ultimatum.

"Marry me, Hanslee, or let's go our separate ways," I protested. But he had no comment.

April 22, 1995, it was 4:06 a.m. in the morning and I could not sleep because I could not stop thinking about what to do to make Hanslee understand that I wanted to live a Christian life. I wrote a prayer in my journal. "Lord, I'm going to walk in faith and tell Hanslee he has to move out or I will. I don't want to live in sin anymore."

It didn't seem right for me to move out of my own home, but I didn't have the courage to tell Hanslee to get out. So, I came up with the craziest idea ever.

When he gets paid, I thought, he'll give me some money. I'll use it to rent an apartment for him.

I found a nice apartment not far from where I lived, and bought furniture from a thrift store. I took Hanslee to work as usual, and then I asked my brother Keith to help me move the furniture to the apartment. Afterward, I mentally rehearsed what I would say to Hanslee when I took him to an unfamiliar place.

I picked him up from work as usual and drove him to the new place. I parked the car, and with a knot in my throat, I said, "I want to show you something."

He followed me up a flight of stairs to the loft apartment located above a small movie theater. Opening the door, I said, "This is your new apartment." I felt as though I was about to fall off the edge of a cliff. He looked around at everything as if he could not believe I would do such a thing. But before he had time to protest, I left.

I still felt the need to take care of him, so I went back the next day. When I arrived, Hanslee was laid out on the sofa sleeping, sweat dripping from his forehead. The clothes he'd had on the day before were lying on the floor. The window was opened, but it still felt hot and muggy. I got a small blue face towel from the bathroom to wipe the sweat from his forehead.

"Hey, Sweets," he said groggily with his eyes still closed.

"I brought you something to eat," I told him.

"Thanks," he replied, but he didn't get up or say anything else, so I left. Each time I went over to visit after that, I found he had not gone to work, but had managed to get wasted.

A few weeks later, Hanslee started coming to visit me. He complained about the heat at his apartment and asked several times if I'd be willing to let him stay with the boys and me. "It's so hot over there," he said.

After several weeks of his complaints, I allowed him to stay, but I also reminded him of his promise to marry me. Drinking always put Hanslee in a conversational mood, and I took the opportunities to bring up the subject of marriage again and again. He seemed unconcerned about that particular subject.

One night, after we'd had a nice day, he decided to top it off with drinking as usual. That's when I brought up the subject once again, hoping the alcohol would do the talking for him.

"Alright, I'll marry you. Set the date," he promised.

The following day I looked at the calendar by myself. A day in July when the sun is shining bright, I thought, would be the perfect day. I called my cousin Penny and asked her to make some invitations. I asked her to make an appointment for premarital counseling for us with her husband, Kevin, who was a minister.

Hanslee really didn't want to go for the counseling, but he went anyway. One evening we went over to Penny's house. She greeted us at the door. "Come on in and have a seat. I'll tell Kevin you are here."

We sat down on the sofa in the living room and Bradrell and Hanslee III went in to the room to play with Penny's kids. While we waited, Hanslee and I stared at each other like we did when we first met.

Kevin came in a couple minutes later and sat in the chair next to the sofa. He asked, "Hanslee, do you want to marry Darlene?"

Hanslee replied, "I really do love Darlene and I want to make her happy. If that's what she wants, then I'll marry her."

Then Kevin talked to me. "Darlene, are you willing to accept Hanslee the way he is? Do you really want to marry him?"

"Yes," I said.

"Marriage is a lot of give and take and a lot of respect for each other," Kevin advised us. I understood what he meant, but I wasn't sure Hanslee did. I was ready to commit to honoring Hanslee as my husband, but I realized later that he had other motives.

The morning of July 29, 1995, I awoke the happiest woman alive, ready to get married and make my relationship with Hanslee legal. I woke him up as I was leaving to go to my sister's to get ready for my wedding. I realized my soon-to-be husband was hung-over. While I slept, I believe he stayed up all night drinking and smoking pot.

"Are you coming?" I asked.

"Where's my money?" he wanted to know, grabbing my arm.

"I told you last night I bought the rings and something for you to wear to our wedding."

"I didn't tell you to spend my money on no wedding. I want my money," he demanded, sitting up on the couch.

I threw what money I had at him and walked out. I got into my car and cried all the way to my sister's. I can't marry him, I told myself, I just can't! Before I went inside I dried away my tears and didn't tell anyone what had happened; I just hoped he would not show up.

When I walked into the house, Bradrell and Hanslee III greeted me with lots of hugs and kisses, as if they really missed me. It was routine for them to spend the night over at my sister's. I felt very fortunate and appreciative when my sister said they could stay. Hanslee could be very unpredictable.

My mother, my sister Loretta, and my best friend Sandra had already prepared everything. They had set up a white heart-shaped wedding arch in Loretta's front yard. The arch was decorated with beautiful pink and white flowers with greenery. A table was set for the food, decorated with a white lace tablecloth and a bouquet of summer flowers. The iron post and railing on the porch were entwined with pink and gray streamers. Everything looked so pretty, meant for a pretty bride.

Sandra, my best friend, was my maid of honor, and my niece Troyetta and little cousin Brittany were the flower girls, dressed up oh-so-pretty. Bradrell stood in as best man and Hanslee III was the ring bearer. They were both dressed in handsome gray suits.

Seeing that everyone except me was dressed, I held back my tears and went in to get ready. The guests were already arriving.

When Gretia came into the room where I was dressing, I asked, "Is he out there?" I was so nervous I could not stop peeking out the window. I prayed, if he shows up, I hope it is because he has changed and truly loves me.

I had been dressed and waiting twenty minutes when someone finally said, "He's here." He must love me, I thought. My palms were sweating like the first time I met him, and I was shaking. My cousin Tammy played the song I had requested, *You'll Always Be My Baby*. I was ready to meet my groom. Charles, my stepfather, took my arm into his and escorted me outside to Hanslee under the arch.

Kevin performed the ceremony and as he led us in our vows I couldn't take my eyes off Hanslee, and he didn't take his eyes off me. I could tell he was still high on booze and pot because his eyes were droopy and red. Tears rolled down my face as I recited my vows. I meant every word I said.

After I said, "Yes," I stood there hoping he would say, "No, I don't promise you anything, Darlene, I just can't." I tried to fight back the thoughts of what he had done to me four hours prior to our wedding, but I couldn't. I cried because I was confused. He had threatened me. He had demanded that I return his money. Deep down in my heart and mind, I felt he couldn't really love me. But he showed up; maybe he was truly sorry for what he had done to me that day and in the past. My thoughts were conflicting with one another.

He said, "Yes, I do," and we were married. He kissed and hugged me tight; it felt very much like love and then we held hands while everyone congratulated us. All my friends from the cell group were there, which made me extremely happy.

The following day we were pulling into my mother's front driveway to visit and I informed Hanslee that I was going to take our marriage documents to the courthouse on Monday of the next week.

He said, "You'd better not take those papers down there. The judge might recognize my name and come and arrest me."

"For what?" I asked.

"You take those papers down there and you'll see what will happen," he said roughly.

At that moment, I felt stupid because I had married someone who really didn't want to marry me.

Later that night I wondered if I should take the papers or not. No, I can't, I said to myself. I'll just divorce him. He can't keep treating me this way.

The next day I called Pierre, a student lawyer at Southern University. "If I don't take my signed marriage paperwork back to the courthouse, is my marriage legal?" I asked him, hoping he would say no, because I did not want to be married to Hanslee at that point.

"Did you stand before a preacher, and did you say your vows?" Pierre asked.

"Yes," I replied.

"Your marriage is legal, but it won't be on file at the courthouse," he informed me. Hearing that, I felt trapped.

I thought there was no way I was going to be unhappy for the rest of my life.

"Can I get it annulled?" I asked.

"No, you would have to file for divorce."

"Thank you," I said, and hung up the phone.

By November of 1995, I was pregnant with my third child. Hanslee and I had been married four months. Only a few things had changed; most things remained the same. Sometimes Hanslee would be very nice to me. He'd cook dinner for the boys and me; he'd play with the children; he'd make me laugh. He even suggested a name for our new baby. He wanted to name our baby Joshua Miguel.

Hanslee loved spending time at my mother's, hanging out with my brother. There were times he'd let me sleep in peace and not bother me if he came in late from my mother's. He would want to make love to me a couple of hours before it was time for him to go to work. These were wonderful moments, especially now that we were married. I didn't have to feel guilty anymore. And before he'd leave for work, he would kiss me goodbye. Those were the things I loved about our marriage and wished it could be like that forever.

In May of 1996 my doctor put me on bed rest because I started having contractions. She told me if I didn't stay off my feet I would risk having the baby early. Hanslee didn't feel I needed the rest. He still expected me to fulfill my wifely duties: to be a mother to him and my children; work a full-time job; cook and clean. Thank God, my mother had the heart to take care of me. She brought me something to eat every day, took care of the children, and cleaned my house.

I had been in bed for about three weeks when Hanslee came into the room one night. He was upset because my mother was using my car.

"Where's the car?" he asked. He sat down at the foot of the bed.

"My mother needed it," I explained.

"I needed it too."

"You wrecked...," I began, reminding him that it was his fault I wouldn't allow him to drive my car. I can't express how furious I was. He had wrecked my car and left the scene of the accident a few weeks prior.

"You have it all mixed up," he countered. "I wouldn't hold anything against you. I wouldn't care if you wrecked my car."

"If you had a driver's license, Hanslee, I wouldn't mind you drive my car." I sat up. "And another thing, you always lie about when you'll be back. I can't trust you."

"I didn't call the cops because I thought they would arrest me." He didn't think I understood his point of view, but I did. "You need help Darlene. Your outlook on life is all messed up." His voice became louder and louder. He complained about how unhappy he was being there with me. Then he left. I lay back down and just prayed that God would help us both.

After awhile, one bad thing led to another. Hanslee started coming home late from work. I started to worry about where he had been.

"The guy I get a ride from had to go somewhere before he could drop me off," he exclaimed after I told him that I would appreciate it if he took the time to call me to let me know he was going to be late.

Dealing with Hanslee was like a living nightmare, and there were nights I couldn't rest. I remember on one particular night, he cussed me out because I didn't want to be bothered. He had been drinking and smoking pot ever since he returned from work. He talked as if the devil was controlling him. I was afraid, so I didn't comment on anything. Finally he left for a while.

I had been wondering where he spent his time when he wasn't at home. I really wanted to ask, but didn't because I knew it would just start an argument. He gave me the impression he was turned off by me, but I yearned for affection even more since I was pregnant. When I tried to touch or hug or kiss him, he'd make excuses to avoid it.

Later that night, when he returned, he had calmed down. "Hey, Sweets, I'm sorry," he said over and over again, trying to get me to believe him. He was like a totally different person. I didn't know if I should tell him to leave and never come back, or say I understood what he was going through. Still afraid of what he might do next, I decided to say nothing. Every time he apologized, he seemed sincere. He talked and talked about a lot of things, but I had no clue what it all meant. Eventually he fell asleep.

I stayed awake all night, worrying about what to do. I wondered what would happen if I left. Would it teach him a lesson and make him realize he shouldn't treat me that way? No, I doubted it. Then I started thinking about the vows I had made before God, "...for better or for worse." That night I turned to the word of God for comfort. I read Psalm 119:132, 134 in my King James Bible. David asked the Lord to have mercy on him and save him from his oppressors. I asked the Lord to do the same for me. This gave me strength to go on.

By June of 1996 I was still struggling with hardcore reality: Hanslee did not love me. My decision to say nothing faded. I wanted to know how he felt about me, so one night when he got into bed I asked, "Don't you love me anymore?"

"I don't love you romantically. I love you like a sister," he said with no explanation. I need a way out, I thought.

Several nights later he came home after I had gone to bed. He sat on the bed, he was very angry. Hanslee started screaming and yelling at me. "Why isn't the car here again? Where is the food I told you to buy?" he asked. It was like he had turned into a madman, and I was afraid he would hurt me. So I sat up in bed, my heart racing and my body shaking. He got up and walked into the kitchen. I got up to go to the rest room where he met me and started yelling again. I was shaking so bad, I did not make it to the toilet. He made me wet my pants.

"You got two dollars?" he asked after I came out of the rest room. I gave him two dollars and he left. I got on my knees and prayed God would protect me, then I fell asleep. I was glad my children were with my mother. The next morning he acted like nothing had ever happened. After that, I couldn't stay in bed like the doctor had ordered.

Realizing that Hanslee was no help, and that he wasn't going to change, I left him and went to live stay with Loretta. She was always willing to take me in, no questions asked.

A week after I left, I found myself crying and regretting my decision to leave him. I wanted to be with him no matter what, and I couldn't understand why. I just knew that I loved him and couldn't live without him. Maybe it was because I was afraid he'd treat someone else better than he treated me. I didn't want that to happen. I wanted to give him another chance to show me he loved me. I called him a few times at his job, just to see if he was still working. I thought this was a good thing because he would be able to pay the rent.

Doctor Rene, my gynecologist, scheduled me for delivery on August 6th because my baby was showing signs of stress. Preoccupied with my relationship with Hanslee,

I missed the appointment. I worried about how he was getting to work. I worried about who he had in my house while I was away.

Curiosity got the best of me. I couldn't rest not knowing how he was getting to work, so I drove to his job site. I parked in the parking lot where he couldn't see me. A strange woman pulled in and dropped him off. I felt like such a fool. So that's where he had been spending his time. She must be the one he had been with all those nights he had been coming home late, I thought.

The next day I confronted him at work. My baby could have come at any time, but I didn't care. I wanted him to know I knew that he must have been seeing that woman for a while if she was giving him rides to work. I went to the front office and asked, "Is it possible for you to call Hanslee? I am his wife, and I need to talk to him."

A man paged him, and I walked outside to wait. Several minutes later Hanslee came out. He had a smirk on his face. "What are you doing here, Darlene? You need to go home."

I saw the woman waiting there to pick him up, and my stomach felt like a ton of bricks. It seemed like when we were in public, he acted as if he was the good guy and I was the crazy one.

"Who is she?" I asked. "I'm not going anywhere until you tell me what's going on. I'm your wife."

"You left me. Now go home."

"No," I protested. "Are you going to give me some money for your baby?"

"Yes, now go home," he replied. His employer gave him his check and sent him home for the day, because I had caused a scene. He got into the car with the woman and they drove away. I followed them to a store where he cashed his check. I waited until he came out to give me some money, then I left.

Doctor Rene rescheduled my delivery date for August 8th. My mother took me to the hospital at 6 a.m. that morning. Bradrell and Hanslee III were allowed to stay in my room until I was ready to give birth to Josh. They were excited about their new baby brother. The nurses gave each one of them a scrub suit and mask. My mother took lots of photos of the boys with their gear on. Seeing them happy made me forget about Hanslee for awhile. But after all the excitement was over and Josh was born, I was so sad. Hanslee wasn't there with our new baby and me. That wasn't the way it was supposed to turn out.

When I got out of the hospital I went to live with my sister again. It had been twenty-three days since I had separated from Hanslee. I continued praying he would straighten up, become a man, and live up to his responsibilities.

At the end of August 1996, Hanslee called me. I told him I was trying to get over him and really didn't want to see him. "If you don't come get me, I won't have a ride home," he said.

"Why isn't your woman giving you a ride home?" I asked. I was excited he had called, but I didn't want to let him know because he might think I was missing him. I would love to see him, I thought. I really did miss him, and now he needed me.

"She let her son use the car to go to New Orleans," he explained. I thought if I helped him, he would treat me better and he'd see that I really did love him. Without any hesitation, I asked my sister to look after my children. Then I picked him up and dropped him off at his friend's house. We didn't say much to each other. I didn't whine and complain. I didn't tell him how much I missed him. I managed to help him in his time of need without expecting anything in return.

A couple of days later, Hanslee called me again from the woman's house. We talked a while about why he wasn't living at home. He said, "You left me, Darlene. What was I supposed to do?"

"Not live with another woman, for sure!" I replied. I wished he had shown me he could stand on his own two feet. I was disappointed he didn't stay in our house, change his attitude, and ask me to come home.

"I'm just renting a room from her," he tried to convince me.

"I'm no fool, Hanslee," I told him.

Several days after that, I called him. The woman told me not to call her house anymore, but I said, "You need to tell Hanslee not to call me if you don't want me calling your house." Two days later he called me from her house again. He wanted me to believe he was not sleeping with her, and that he was paying her to take him to work.

The next day I called him again and the woman answered the phone. "Lee isn't here. I thought I told you not to call my house," she said.

"Hanslee called me and I'm returning his call. He said he's renting a room from you. So you're saying your tenant can't receive phone calls."

"Hanslee sleeps with me every night," she countered.

"I wonder why he's telling me something different. You might want to ask him. Sounds like to me he's trying to keep a door open here with his wife."

"Just don't call here anymore," she demanded, and hung up the phone.

Hanslee called me the next day and I told him what the woman said. He still tried to deny what was going on over there with her. Suddenly he said, "I'll call you back."

A few minutes after I hung up the phone, the woman called. We had a long conversation, and then she ended it by saying, "You can have your husband back. I don't want him." An hour later, she brought all of his things to me at my sister's house. I put them in the trunk of my car because I really didn't know what else to do with them. I felt like such a fool for allowing this to happen to me.

The woman must have put Hanslee out because he called me a week later. He wanted to know if it was okay for him to sleep in my car. I agreed because I felt sorry for him in some way, and the love I had in my heart for him was deeper than I could ever understand. After that I saw him a couple of times, then he disappeared for a while.

By the time I heard from him again, I had moved into a house on Osborne Avenue. He came by my mother's house to visit and to apologize. He seemed to love spending time with Josh, who was four months old at the time. I enjoyed seeing them together too, so I allowed him back into my life.

Contemplating Murder

December 5, 1996, was Hanslee's 34th birthday. After his birthday party at my mother's, I sensed he was very unhappy. I left the kids with my mother so Hanslee and I could spend some romantic time together, but Hanslee had other plans. He begged me to let him use my car. I knew deep down in my gut I shouldn't, but I did anyway, just so he would leave me alone. He promised he would be right back.

He showed up six hours later. He was drunk and high on drugs, and I knew I shouldn't say anything to him about where he had been in my car or what took him so long to come home.

"Are you mad at me?" he asked with an angry attitude.

"No," I replied.

"Because if you are, I don't give a ....!" he cursed.

"That's fine," I said, hoping he wouldn't start anything with me. But he kept on and on until I told him how I felt. As soon as I spoke, he began slapping me in the face until I could not see straight. I did not fight back because I thought it would make things worse.

After beating me, he said, "You can leave now, I don't give a ....! I don't want you here anyway!" He walked around the house, huffing and puffing like he owned the place. He finished his drink, laid down on the sofa, and talked about what he was going to do to my brother, Keith. He said he would hurt him very badly one day. I wasn't sure why he was so angry with my brother.

In the meantime I was trying to stop crying. I was confused about whether or not to leave right then. When I realized he had fallen asleep, I started getting ready to leave. I put some of our clothes in a basket. I went to the cabinet to grab my baby's milk and saw the hammer he used at work. For an instant, I thought about what I could do with that hammer. I picked it up and said to myself, I could take this ... hammer and beat his ... brains out of his head (my words were very profane). But God was watching over me that night.

Seconds after that thought, God spoke to me by His Spirit and said, "What about your children? You will end up in jail if you do that. He is not worth it." I placed the hammer back into the cabinet. Breathing deeply, I fell on my knees with my face to the floor and cried.

Even though I had thanked God for saving me, I felt really bad that I had allowed Hanslee to hurt me and get away with it. I got up off my knees, got into my bed and cried much harder. After a while, I calmed down and then I thought of a plan to get away from him. I knew when he woke up he would apologize for what he had done to me. Sure enough, he woke up four hours later and he asked me to forgive him. I did, but just to buy some time.

That morning I was surprised he was willing to go to work, but I was glad for it. While thinking about my plans to escape his madness and cruelty, I took him to work like a wife should when there is only one car. He kissed me goodbye and said, "I'm sorry, please forgive me. I love you. I get off at 4:30. Are you coming to get me?"

I was speechless at first, because I couldn't believe I was going through with my plans. I was anxious but confident. "Okay," was all I could force out. I couldn't seem to pull away fast enough after that. I headed straight to my mother's house.

I told my mother Hanslee had slapped me. I asked her and brother, Keith to help me move my stuff out of my house. I didn't tell my brother why I wanted to move, because I knew he would want to beat Hanslee up. I figured we could do it before he came home from work. My brother reluctantly agreed, saying, "I don't understand why you keep moving. You need to stay where you are and stop moving so much." After they agreed to help me, I took the kids to Loretta's house.

At 4:30 p.m., we were just finishing up and I thought about Hanslee. I had made up my mind the night before I wasn't going to be there to pick him up from work. I'm free, I thought to myself, and I didn't plan on going back.

My conscience tried to make me feel sorry for him, but I let reality guide me this time. All day, I forced myself not to worry about how he would react to what I had done or where he would live. I picked my kids up from my sister's and went back to my mother's. Bradrell and Hanslee III played outside while I bonded with Josh. My mother cooked dinner for us and we ate.

At 10:30 p.m., Hanslee showed up at my mother's house looking for me. "Lee's out there," my brother informed me.

I was nervous and not sure what to say to him. I can't tell him, I thought. I went outside to see what he wanted.

"Why didn't you pick me up?" he wanted to know.

"I thought maybe you could get a ride home with one of the guys at work," I replied.

"Can you come take me home?" he asked.

"Okay," I said. I went back into the house and told my mother I would be right back. We arrived at the house within five minutes. He got out, walked to the door and unlocked it. I drove off and went back to my mother's. When I got there, I picked Josh up, held him close, kissed him and whispered, "I love you so much." I sensed Bradrell and Hanslee III wanted some attention too, so I asked them to give me a hug, and told them I loved them very, very much.

After about a week of staying with my mother, I realized I really didn't want to live there. She had a new husband, and my brother was not easy to get along with. I called the battered women's hot-line number to ask for help. They referred me to the Zunta House. I called Zunta House and they gave me an appointment date to check in.

I tried staying at the shelter, but it didn't last. It was cold during the night, and I wasn't sure if the heat was working or not. Our room was located on the second floor, and had two twin beds and a mirror-less dresser. They gave us two sheets, one fitted and one flat, for each of the beds. Bradrell and Hanslee shared one of the twin beds. Josh had a baby bed but I let him sleep with me. The mattresses were the stiff plastic kind with cracks in them. The plastic poked me and made it difficult to sleep. The restroom was down the hall from our room. I didn't like not having my own place to shower. The kitchen was downstairs on the first floor. I must say, the food the women took turns preparing was delicious.

Bradrell and Hanslee III seemed to be okay with the situation because they didn't complain at all. They enjoyed playing with the other kids in the shelter.

Unable to bear those conditions, I asked Loretta if we could live with her for a while. She agreed yet again. Quite often when I went to my mother's, Hanslee would be there. He'd want to chat and see the kids. My mother told me the reason she allowed Hanslee to come to see me at her house was because she felt it was up to me to tell him not to come.

Eventually I told him he had until the end of the month to find another place to live because I had to turn the keys to the house back in. Knowing he didn't have anywhere to go, I suggested he talk to my cousin Cookie to see if he could rent a room from her. Hanslee talked to her and she allowed him to move in the next day.

After several weeks, the situation was not working out at my cousin's house, so I convinced him to move into the two-story house across the street from her. He moved in and ended up liking the place.

Even though Hanslee had his own place, he spent a lot of his time at my mother's. He called me from her house one night at about 9:20 p.m. "Are you coming to take me home?"

Somehow I forgot about why I had left him. He would not go away. I don't know why I felt the need to help him every time we were separated. "Okay, I guess so," I told him. I finished watching the movie I had started, then fixed a bottle for Josh. I gave the bottle to Loretta and told her I would be right back.

When I arrived, he wasn't ready, as usual. He was watching TV, because he didn't have one in his house, and eating as if he hadn't eaten in days. When the show was over, he started messing with my brother's VCR.

"I thought you were ready to go," I protested.

"I am!" he replied, but continued to mess with the VCR for another 25 minutes. As we were leaving, Anthony drove up. Hanslee jumped out of the car, forgot all about me, and stood there talking. I thought he was going to leave with Anthony, but eventually he got back in the car and we left.

We finally arrived at his house at 10:45. "Are you going to light the heater?" I asked. "It's cold in here." I went upstairs, thinking we would spend some time together. The bed was a mess, and as I began making it up, I found a piece of a condom package. I began to wonder if Hanslee was bisexual. But he couldn't be – he had told me he detested homosexuals. The thought of him in bed with Anthony made my stomach turn. I became weaker the longer I thought about it. Anthony had been to prison several times. He acted like he could have been someone's boyfriend in jail. I looked for more pieces of the package.

First, I looked in Hanslee's pants pocket, but found nothing. Next, I looked around and noticed a broken antenna with a piece of wire stuffed in one end lying on his dresser. (I learned this was a type of pipe for smoking crack.) He'd been doing drugs again, I guessed. How am I going to ask him about this stuff, I wondered. I said to myself, I'm not going to mention it at all. He doesn't seem like he has anything to hide. But then I thought, no, I must say something.

"Somebody's been using LifeStyles, I see," I commented. But he had already undressed and gotten into bed, and didn't hear a word I said. I really wanted to go off on him, but I didn't. What if he was bisexual – would I still love him? I really preferred not to know. But he couldn't have had a woman over here unless Anthony brought her. I thought about it over and over.

Suddenly Hanslee got up and began to put his clothes back on. "Where are you going?" I asked.

"Downstairs, to turn the water on," he replied. He had to turn the water on to flush the toilet, then turn it off again when he was done because there was a water leak somewhere under the house.

I noticed he was putting on the pants I had found the pipe in. "Those are not the pants you had on," I pointed out.

"Oh," he said as he checked the pockets, and then went downstairs. But it sounded like he stopped in the living room instead of going outside to turn on the water. I didn't hear the door open. If that pipe is not in there when I check again, I'll know he is doing drugs again. I'm not going to associate with him as long as he is doing drugs, I thought.

What is taking him so long, I whispered to myself. I was expecting him to come up and spend some time with me before I left. I went downstairs to see what he was doing. He had taken off his clothes and was lying on the sofa. I sat in a chair nearby and asked him to explain why he was ignoring me. He didn't answer, so I checked for the pipe again and it was still there. Why? I thought. Why is he hurting himself with that stuff? I placed the pipe back into his pocket and left.

A couple of nights later, I gave him a ride again. Before we left he asked me to fix him a plate to take with him. He ate it on the way to his house. After he was done with it, he complained that it was a child's plate —not enough for him.

When I tried to explain there was only a little food left, he began slapping me as I was parking the car. Then he threw the plate and what was left in it at me. He complained about my brother and said one day he was going to kill him. As soon as he got out of the car, I put the car in reverse. I yelled at him, "Don't you ever come looking for me again!" I couldn't believe I had allowed him to treat me that way again.

Treatment: Can it Change Him?

By the time I heard from Hanslee again, I had moved from Loretta's house and had been in my own apartment on McClelland Avenue for six months. I was at Loretta's doing my laundry when he called me. "Hey, Sweets, can you come pick me up?" he asked.

"From where?" I wanted to know. I was very surprised, but glad to hear from him. I wondered. Why is he calling me? Maybe this time he'll see that I love him if I help out.

"Baton Rouge Health Unit," he replied.

I put another load of clothes in the washer, told my sister I would be right back, and asked her to watch the kids for me.

"Where are you going?" she asked.

"I'll be right back," I repeated. I didn't give her a chance to lecture me; I left to pick him up.

When I saw him I noticed he had gained weight and looked very handsome, as if he had been taking care of himself.

"Where have you been?" I inquired as he got into the car. My curiosity was raging; I needed to know where he had been all that time. He looked and smelled different, but I feared it could be just a front.

"In treatment," he replied, sounding extremely upbeat. "Hey, Sweets, I can get a job in Mobile, Alabama. I was wondering if you could loan me some money for a bus ticket."

"I'll have to think about it," I replied, wondering if he was really telling the truth. I dropped him off at his friend's house.

Two days later Hanslee showed up at my mother's, still looking good and nicely put together, expecting me to loan him the money to go to Mobile, three hours from Baton Rouge. Overwhelmed by the way he looked, but not willing to give him the money, I agreed to take him to Mobile.

Later that night, he asked if he could stay one last night at my place. He promised me he would not come back because he was moving to Mobile. He promised to send money to help with the kids, so I agreed, hoping he would live up to his promises. That night the kids, Hanslee, and I went home. After the kids were asleep, Hanslee and I made love. I forgot about all the bad things he had done to me, and began hoping for a new start in our relationship.

The next morning I took Bradrell and Hanslee III to school and Josh to my mother's. Then I took Hanslee to Mobile to apply for a job. I didn't tell my mother where I was going because I knew she would try to stop me.

When we got to Mobile Hanslee found out he needed his social security card. We ended up going back to Mobile two more times before he got the job. He worked for a couple of months and faithfully sent me the money he had promised. Then all of a sudden he called and wanted me to pick him up because he was sick. After I picked him up from Mobile, his life began to go downhill. He had been drinking and doing drugs while he was in Mobile. I tried all I could to make things work with Hanslee, but he wanted to do things his way.

When Hanslee had been back home with us a month, I allowed him to use my car and he stayed out until the next morning. I told him I was not going to put up with his mess anymore.

I said, "If you stay out like that again—don't come back." But in spite of my warning, he stayed out again, and this time when he came back, someone had busted out the passenger window of my car. I was furious, but I didn't let him know because I knew it would start a big one-way fight. He apologized and promised to pay to get the window fixed. I tried not to let it worry me and didn't say anymore about it. I knew he wasn't going to get it fixed, so I filed a claim with the insurance company.

For the third time, he left and didn't come home until three a.m. I heard a knock at the door. Although I knew it was him, I asked, "Who is it?"

"It's me, Sweets," he said from the other side of the door.

Pacing back and forth I said, "Go away, Hanslee! You don't love me; you just want to make me miserable." Next thing I knew, he was pounding on the door, demanding to be let in. I had wired the door shut with a hanger, before he arrived. He kicked on it several times. I began to panic a little, wondering what to do. Thank God my kids were at my sister's. "If you don't go away, I'm calling the police!" I yelled. He kicked a few more times, so I picked up the phone and called the police.

By the time the police came, Hanslee was gone. The police asked the routine questions and saw that Hanslee must have been very upset. They noticed the condition of the door and made a note for the police report. The door frame was cracked and he had kicked the door so hard he left his footprint in it. If it weren't for God giving me the idea to use the hanger, no telling what he would have done to me that morning.

Don't die for Love Don't die for Love
If you're in love and it's causing you pain
Escape the shame
Don't die for love Don't die for love
If you're not respected for the love you give
Leave the pain
Escape the shame
Don't die for Love Don't die for Love
There's another looking for love to respect
Leave the pain
Escape the shame
Live for love Live for love
Don't die for love Don't die for love
Live for love

D.F.D. Nance, July 25, 1996

Dying for Love

After that night, I moved back with Loretta for a while because I was afraid Hanslee would come back asking me to give him another chance. I promised myself again I would not allow him to mess up what I had been working very hard to achieve.

Hanslee still came to my mother's house to visit. Each time I saw him he'd apologize, and each time my heart began to forgive and to forget. After a while I desired to be with him again, because when he made love to me I felt as though he really cared about me. He seemed like another person, very gentle. I moved into another house on Monroe Avenue and allowed him to move back in with the kids and me. I made it clear that I wasn't going to let him abuse me.

But things didn't get any better, and I began to think about how my relationship with Hanslee was affecting my children. I noticed that Hanslee picked fights with me even when the children were around. So I decided that if things didn't change soon, I was going to leave for good.

Then, one night in March of 1999, Hanslee came home very late, something he had promised he would never do again. I decided to sleep on the couch that night, because I didn't want to sleep with him. I put on a pair of sweat pants and t-shirt because I had a feeling he was going to pick a fight with me.

"Hey, Sweets, wake up," he said as he sat down on the couch beside me.

"Leave me alone," I responded.

"What? You mad at me?" he asked.

"Could you please leave me alone?" I insisted. "I just want to go to sleep."

"I'll beat your (blank) all over this living room," he threatened loudly.

Josh (almost three years old at this time) woke up and stood up in his bed. He held out his hands and said, "Mommy." I took him, sleepy-eyed, out of his bed and set him down on the couch beside me. Bradrell (now 11 years old) and Hanslee III (9) were still asleep in their beds.

"Hanslee, if you hit me, you'd better kill me," I said.

"I'm not going to hit you. Can we...?" he said, as he rubbed my legs. He smelled like vomit and alcohol.

"I don't feel like it right now," I insisted. He touched my leg again and again, and I moved his hand away each time. "I don't know where you've been. You don't have any respect for me. You don't love me. I thought you weren't going to stay out late anymore."

"I haven't been with another woman," he tried to explain.

"I don't care, you haven't been here with me," I replied. I turned away from him and that made him very angry.

"You think you're better than me. I don't even know why I came back here, knowing I didn't want you. You ain't nothing but a (blank). You ain't no show-pony. I can have one, you know. If I leave you, nobody is going to want you. I stay here because I feel sorry for you." He went on and on, trying to make me feel bad. "You just don't know, but I could have beaten you're a..!"

I sat up and picked up the wrench that was lying on the coffee table. "Leave me alone! You better not hit me!" I protested. Bradrell and Hanslee III woke up.

"Put the wrench down! Put it down!" he kept demanding.

"If you hit me, Hanslee, I – I'll... I'm tired of you treating me any old kind of way!"

Josh was still sitting on the sofa. "Put the wrench down, Mommy!" he cried.

Hanslee slapped me in the face and grabbed me. I screamed, "Leave me alone!"

While he was trying to hold me down, I managed (I believe God gave me the strength) to hit him in the head with that wrench several times. I broke free and grabbed Josh and ran out the front door to my car. Bradrell and Hanslee III were still in their beds.

"Bradrell, Hanslee!" I shouted as I started the car. "Come on and get into the car!" In the past I had left Bradrell behind because Hanslee would not let me take him. He had to keep something that belonged to me so I would have to come back. But this time I was not leaving them behind.

Hanslee stood on the top steps of the house, still stunned, staggering, blood dripping from his head. "Look what you've done to me!" he yelled.

Bradrell and Hanslee III hesitated for a moment. "Come on. Don't be scared," I encouraged them, and they ran and got in the car. Then I drove to my mother's house and told her what had happened. About ten minutes later I heard a knock at the door. My mother answered the door; it was Hanslee.

"I need to talk to Darlene," he said.

"Lee, you need to just go home," my mother advised him.

"I need to talk to her," he insisted.

I went outside in spite of my mother's warning, because I wanted him to just leave me alone. He cursed me out in front of my mother, then left very upset. Less than fifteen minutes later we heard the sound of a car crash close by and went outside to see what had happened. There was Hanslee again, and he had run into my car which was parked in my mother's driveway.

I called the police but they didn't do anything about it. The officer asked, "Are you married to him?"

"Yes," I replied.

"Louisiana is a community property state, which means whatever belongs to you also belongs to him," the policeman explained. He said Hanslee could tear the car up if he wanted to. This really upset me because I had worked hard to pay for that car, and I knew Hanslee wasn't going to pay to get it fixed.

The next morning Hanslee called me. "I could have pressed charges against you for busting my head open," he complained.

"I don't care. Don't call me anymore," I replied, and hung up the phone. But a couple of days later he came to my mother's house to apologize. I tried to accept his apology, but he was arrogant with Bradrell for no reason at all. I can't remember what he said, but I knew he had no right to talk to him that way. Watching him act this way, I thought to myself, oh no, this is the last straw. I will not allow him to abuse my children, and I will not allow him to abuse me ever again. At that moment I became brave and demanded that he leaves and never come back.

<u>A New Start</u>

Don't be afraid of a new start
It's okay if you have to start over again
Learn from your mistakes
Try not to make them again
Trust God and know
God is with you always
Everything's going to be alright

D.F.D. Nance, April 8, 1999

The Big Move

The next day I was watching the "700 Club" on TV and saw a lady telling her story about being abused by her husband. She said he almost killed her several times. She made up her mind she would not let him kill her. She said she called the battered women's 1-800 number and got help. She left him and wrote a book about what happened to her. She got married again, and her new husband treats her with respect. This gave me a little hope; my life wasn't over after all.

A couple of days later I was sitting on the sofa at my mother's watching the six o'clock news. The report was about a woman, her mother, and her two-year-old child, who had been shot down by her husband while they attended church. He was upset because she had filed for divorce. The news reporter also encouraged other women to call the 1-800 number to get help if they were experiencing any type of abuse.

Even though I had left Hanslee, I became afraid. What if my husband came and did the same thing to my family and me? I called the 1-800 number and asked for help. I didn't want to go back to him, and I knew if I didn't get help I would.

Loretta allowed us to stay with her until a room at Zunta House, the domestic violence shelter, became available. I called three or four times and finally was told there was a vacancy.

During the intake, I asked them if they could help me relocate because I was afraid I would go back to him. They said, "Yes, where would you like to go?"

I replied, "Kansas City, Missouri," because I had relatives there.

My case manager gave me the information about a shelter there, Newhouse. I contacted Newhouse, a residential center for battered women, and arranged reservations for the move to Kansas City. When I called, everyone I talked to seemed very nice and professional. They said I could get lots of help from the program. I was scared to drive all the way to Kansas City by myself, but I prayed that God would help me to arrive safely. I was unable to leave right away because my car was still being repaired.

The two months I stayed at Zunta House seemed like the longest two months of my life. There were times I wanted to give up and go back home to Hanslee, but thankfully God gave me the strength to move forward. I didn't tell anyone about my plans to leave until the day I was to depart. I felt that if I told anyone, they would have tried to stop me – not because they didn't want the best for me, but because they loved me and would hate to see me leave.

My mother and sister were very sad to hear I was leaving. They wanted me to reconsider. They suggested I leave the children, thinking it would be easier to start over without them. I believe they meant well, but I just couldn't leave them behind, so I took them with me to make a new life for us. I drove nine hundred miles away from the place I had called home for thirty-three years, with just my children and a few items that were dear to me. This would turn out to be the best decision I would ever make in my life.

I arrived in Kansas City on April 18, 1999, at 10:45 p.m. The shelter's advocate greeted me with a warm welcome, and then directed us to a huge dining room area. After we finished eating, she took us on a tour and showed us our room. It was a nice place.

We had a great view of the outdoors. We could see the children's play area and a main thoroughfare. Each one of us had our own bunk bed. Oh, I felt blessed; I was able to have a private room while some of the smaller families had to share rooms.

Since it was so late, the shelter advocate asked me for basic information and told me my case manager would do an intake the next morning. During the intake, I learned the rules of the shelter. She told me I would attend a lot of mandatory meetings at the center, a program which would help my healing process to begin. I attended group sessions on domestic violence, red flags of abusers, and many other topics. I learned about the cycle of violence, what leads to being in an abusive relationship, codependent behaviors that had to change, the profile and psychiatric diagnosis of many batterers, and anger as it relates to batterers and their victims. I also learned how I had been projecting my anger and frustration onto my children, because of how I was being abused by my husband, and that my codependency stemmed from not having a father in my life when I was a child.

Codependency in unhealthy relationships means that no matter how a person treats you, you accept him or her in your life anyway, because you have no self-esteem. You feel unworthy of respect and allow a person to convince you no one else wants you. Not having a father also led me to have a profound feeling of abandonment. I really didn't know what a healthy male/female relationship looked like. I knew my mother had been in an abusive relationship, and later learned that my maternal grandmother had been, as well.

I knew my faith in God was going to be my only hope. When I began the individual therapy with Eva Howard, she allowed me to express my faith in God and prayed with me many times. After leaving church, I thought what a blessing to feel God's presence in the shelter – the presence of the Holy Spirit. Miss Eva encouraged me to continue seeking a deeper relationship with the Lord. It was the most important part of my shelter stay; without the encouragement, I knew I would have gone back to my abuser. I think it is extremely important for every woman who is in the process of leaving an abusive relationship to find a worship place and make a spiritual commitment to God. It is vital to have fellowship with other believers during this time.

As I took advantage of the opportunities the shelter program offered, I saw how some of the other residents appeared ungrateful and weren't serious about change. I am very grateful to Newhouse administration and staff; they played a huge part in my successful escape from the cycle of violence.

Even though I was comfortable at Newhouse, I became homesick. It got even worse after talking with my mother for the first time after leaving Baton Rouge.

Homesick: Will I Survive?

When I talked to my mother, she said that Hanslee had been looking for me, and that she had been feeding him because she felt God would want her to. He was homeless again. Tears welled in my eyes as she told me about him being there. I had to express how I felt about that. "It's not fair. He's the one who hurt me; he should have been the one to leave. Why did I have to leave?" I complained. But she encouraged me to be strong, saying everything would be okay. There were times when I wanted to just give up and go back home. But I talked to the women's therapist about my feelings. After processing those feelings, I was able to move on. I believe it is very important to have individual and group therapy as a battered woman; group therapy especially helps each person feel less isolated, thinking they are the only one with this problem.

I had been in the shelter four weeks and now began to seek housing and employment. When I left Louisiana, I had my income tax refund to use for travel. Now it had run out, and I needed more money for gas to look for a job and a place to live. Systems, Inc., (an agency that helps with work transportation) helped me with a gas card.

By July 1999 I had found a place and moved in. But by December 14th, I felt homesick again. I had such a strong desire to go back to Baton Rouge. I tried my best to count my blessings, but I still had the blues. I really missed my mother, sister, and brother. Winter was just around the corner when I got a call from my Aunt Dot. When she heard my voice, she became very concerned about me. "What's the matter?" she asked.

"I want to come home," I answered, fighting back my tears.

"It's just the weather. It's because it's cold and dreary in Kansas City. You'll feel different as soon as the summertime rolls around. Then you can come home to visit. I know you don't want to come here and lose what you have over there," she comforted me. I felt encouraged and it helped me to think positively about my situation.

Finally, September rolled around and I had the chance to go home for a week. That's when I realized nothing had changed at home, and I really was in a better place. I went back to Kansas City with my mind made up that I had a few things to accomplish. In August I had started attending college at UMKC, working toward a Bachelor's degree in accounting. I also had a job waiting for me when I got back.

On December 15th, Hanslee III woke me up with an excited, "It's my birthday, Mother!" It was his tenth birthday, and I felt so bad that he'd had to remind me of his special day. It hurt me that I couldn't afford to buy him any presents, but thank God, Hanslee wasn't too worried about it. Bradrell and Josh helped me sing happy birthday to him. He seemed like the happiest kid on earth, with just a simple song.

My mother called that morning to wish Hanslee III a happy birthday, and to see how we were doing. After she talked to my son, he handed me the phone. "Has Hanslee called or come by?" I asked with the anticipation that she would say yes.

"No," she replied.

"I wish he would send me some money so I could buy our children something for Christmas and for Hanslee III's birthday," I said. "I dreamed about him twice this week."

"What happened?" she asked.

"In the first dream he was still acting like he had not changed, but in the second dream, he had changed and was treating me better," I explained.

"Oh," she replied.

"How are Keith and Charles?" I asked.

"They're doing okay."

"And Loretta?" I continued.

"She's doing okay, too. She wants to give me some money for a bus ticket to come visit you and the boys for Christmas."

On December 23rd I received a call from my mother at 6:45 p.m. "Why aren't you here to pick me up?" she asked.

I was so excited she was able to come! Bradrell asked, "Who is that?"

I wanted it to be a surprise, so I didn't answer him. But Hanslee III yelled from his room, "It's Momo!"

Then I told the boys I would be right back. I took Josh with me to the bus station to pick up my mother. She had lots of stuff with her, and she looked tired. I hugged her with Josh in my arms, and she kissed and hugged both of us. She went to the concession stand at the bus terminal and got a cup of coffee, then said, "Let's go! I'm ready to see my other babies!"

It was the best Christmas present my sons could ever have, their grandmother. She gave all of them hugs and kisses. They all tried to talk to her at once, trying to make up for lost time. "Don't crowd her," I scolded them.

"That's okay," she said, assuring me that she had been looking forward to their hugs. "Did you cook?" she asked.

"Yes," I replied.

"I guessed it was your voice on the phone, Momo," said Hanslee III.

Later, she took a bath while I warmed up the food. We all sat down and ate supper together like old times. As we ate, I forgot about being homesick. I thought about how nice it was to have my own mother at my new home where I had made a fresh start without Hanslee.

On May 25th, 2000, my children and I took another trip to Baton Rouge for a week. We hadn't seen our family for more than a year, so when we arrived, everyone was glad to see us. I was happy to be back at home again.

Loretta looked at me with amazement because I had gained about 22 pounds. She said I looked very happy, and everyone agreed that I looked good. My mother cried when she saw the boys, because she had missed them so much and they had changed a lot. They all were amazed at how much Bradrell had grown. He was taller than everybody except my cousin Mark. I thought my children would enjoy a long summer vacation, so I left them in Baton Rouge and returned to Kansas City alone.

By June, my longing to be with my family and children was plaguing me. I couldn't stop thinking about my family. I wondered what they were doing. I remembered the times I had complained about not having any time to myself, and now I regretted feeling that way. I promised myself that when they did come home, I would try to have more patience with them, and nurture them as a mother should. I prayed that God would help me be more kind to them. I thought about how very much I loved them. They were the reason I chose to live. I also thought about their future, and prayed God would bless their lives with genuine friends and good loving wives who would encourage them in the things they desired to do.

That summer, while my kids were away, I met Luana while attending Sheffield Family Life Center church. I was volunteering in the children's ministry. We became church buddies, and she helped me get through the summer without my children.

Being alone with my thoughts, I begun thinking about my marriage again and what I was going to do about it. I prayed and prayed about it, wondering if I should continue waiting for Hanslee to change his ways.

On July 9th, Loretta called and said Hanslee had left a number for me to call him. I was hesitant to call him, even though I had looked forward to the day he would call. I finally gave in to my curiosity and dialed his number.

"Do you need some money?" he asked, even though he must have known the answer. I played along with his little game, just to see what he was up to.

"Yes, I'll always need money from you because I have your children, and you need to help me take care of them," I answered calmly.

"Well, you need to let me come live with you," he demanded.

I listened to him ramble on and on for a few minutes, realizing he was trying to run the same old games. After I told him he could not come live with me, he began saying mean things about my family. In the background, I could hear a woman's voice demanding he let her use the phone. He told her she would have to wait. He then told me if I did not allow him to come live with me, he could not give me any money.

"Hanslee, how can you tell me to let you come live with me while you are living with another woman right now?" I asked, very disturbed by what he was saying. "I have been waiting for you to change, but you'll never change," I continued.

"You should've stopped waiting for me to change a long time ago. I've been waiting on you, but I'm not going to wait any longer," he said loudly.

"You don't have to wait for me to change, and I don't care anymore!" I cried. "You don't care about us, because if you did, you wouldn't be living with another woman. I haven't let any men come live with me!"

"If you want a divorce," he replied, "I'll sign the papers. Just send them to me when you get them ready!" Then he hung up the phone. I began praising God for His answer to my prayer, showing me that Hanslee was not going to change.

Previously, a friend of mine had told me how she used a divorce kit to obtain her divorce. I was skeptical, but a few weeks later I went to Office Depot and purchased a divorce kit for myself. I held on to it, still hoping for a miracle in my marriage.

But after that phone call with Hanslee, I realized there would be no miracle. He had not changed, nor did he seem to want to. I decided the time had come to open the divorce kit. But the information seemed too complicated, so I put it aside.

In August, I drove back to Baton Rouge to pick up my sons, and my mother came back with us to Kansas City. She came to help look after the boys while I worked and went to school full time. Without her I couldn't have managed. By that time, I had moved to Shawnee, Kansas, and the boys had to adjust to yet another new place.

As March 2001 approached, I worried about what I would do after my mother went back to Baton Rouge. I thought about moving back with her. I could have finished college at Louisiana State University or Northwestern University of Louisiana, but I realized I really didn't want to do that. I asked myself, what would I do about my class? Who would look after Josh? I couldn't leave him with Bradrell and Hanslee III; they were just babies themselves. Another option would be to just take one or two classes at a time, but I figured that would take me forever to graduate. I was in a dilemma; I really didn't know what I was going to do after my mother left.

I decided to contact my therapist from Newhouse, Eva Howard, to help me make the decision. We met for lunch at the Sheraton Hotel on the Plaza in Kansas City. I showed her that my hair was thinning on top because of the stress. I told her if returned to Baton Rouge and sold my car, I could lessen my expenses and ride the bus to Southern University. My mother would be able to help me by looking after my children. Also, Hanslee was not in Baton Rouge, but had gone to New Jersey, so it was safe. She prayed for me to get direction from God to know what to do.

I was feeling sick a lot during that time. Knowing it was due to stress; I prayed God would give me the strength to go on. I started thinking about my marriage again. Should I divorce Hanslee? I still wanted to be with him, and I missed the good times we had together. On the other hand, I felt marrying Hanslee was the biggest mistake I had ever made in my life. I found it hard to forgive myself for that mistake and to just go on with my life. I asked God to forgive me for not listening to His warning signs. My feelings for Hanslee caused confusion in my mind. I knew divorce was wrong, and I desired to love and stay with him until death do us part, but at the same time I was afraid to go back to him. I just wanted to have peace about it.

May 30th that same year, I began to rethink my plans to travel to Baton Rouge in June. I asked myself again and again, should I go home? Finally, I decided to remain in Shawnee, Kansas. It was a hard decision. I saw a lot of opportunities for my sons and myself. I could graduate from UMKC and my children would get a decent education in Johnson County schools. I wouldn't have to worry about getting into arguments with my family about how I should raise my children. Besides, I really liked living in Kansas.

After taking my mother back to Baton Rouge, I began to be really concerned about Hanslee III. The kids at his school had been teasing him during the 2000-2001 school year. He told the counselors the kids made fun of his goal to learn to read better. He didn't handle the teasing well.

That summer he started hanging out with a boy who talked him into doing bad things. They went to a grocery store and stole some things. I thank God the manager called me instead of calling the police. I really didn't know what to do, so I called Loretta. I asked her if he could come out there to live with her for a while, and she agreed. As I watched the plane take off with my eleven-year-old son, I prayed I was not making a mistake in sending him away. Loretta enrolled him in school and took care of him, and he got along fine.

Murder in New Jersey

After Hanslee III left, things went back to normal for a while. I started to relax and enjoy life. But then, on November 26th, 2001, when I returned a call from my sister, my relaxing days came to a halt.

"The police came looking for your Lee," my sister said in a strained voice.

"For what?" I inquired. My hands trembled.

"For murdering a lady," she answered.

"Murdering a lady!" I repeated almost without breathing.

"What do you mean? What did the police say?"

"Only that Lee is a suspect for killing somebody in New Jersey."

I was stunned with disbelief, not able to move. I sat there at the foot of my bed in a daze for several seconds.

That night I could hardly sleep. The quietness brought many thoughts and questions. Was Hanslee capable of committing murder? I couldn't imagine him doing such a thing. I thought about the woman who may have died by the hands of the man I loved so deeply. What could he have done to her? My heart ached as if I knew the woman, as if she was a part of my family. My heart ached for Hanslee because I still loved him so much. How could he? He had to have lost his mind. He couldn't have done it! My thoughts raced in circles.

On November 28th, I received a call from a police department in New Jersey. "Do you know where Hanslee is?" a detective asked.

"No," I answered.

"When was the last time you saw him?" the questions continued.

"I haven't seen him in almost three years now," I replied.

"When was the last time you talked to him?"

"I haven't talked to him in a while," I said.

"Please call me if Hanslee tries to contact you, no matter what time of day it is," the detective instructed me tensely.

Several weeks later I received a letter from my sister containing the newspaper article about Hanslee. As I read the article I couldn't help but think about what might have happened to me. I asked myself, what if I had gone back to him? Would he have killed me? The thoughts became extremely scary.

'Til Death Do Us Part or Divorce

On January 22nd, 2002, the day before my divorce hearing, I started thinking really hard about how I felt about being married. I knew Hanslee wouldn't be there. At one time, I wished he would show up and say he loved me and didn't want a divorce. But things had changed. I still loved him, but I knew I didn't want to be his wife anymore. I had wished for 18 years that he would accept me as his wife, but not anymore. I knew now that was one wish that would never come true. I couldn't trust him to treat me with respect. I couldn't trust him not to hit me ever again, or call me ugly names. I couldn't trust him to care about my feelings. I couldn't trust him to take care of me as a husband should take care of his wife. I couldn't trust him to care about our children. I couldn't trust him not to make me cry and gloat about it. I couldn't trust him to say he was sorry and mean it.

It all seemed too simple. On January 23rd, 2002, I went to the courthouse for the final judgment of my divorce. Still, the doubt set in again. Was I doing the right thing? I remembered telling the Lord that if he allowed me to marry Hanslee, I would never get a divorce. Yet here I was, doing just that.

"Am I late?" I asked my attorney as I arrived at the courthouse.

"No, you're okay," she answered politely. "We just need to go over your divorce papers so that I can get the judge to sign them and then you will be divorced." She explained to me what the divorce papers stated. I agreed to every part of it except the part to change my name back to Dunn. I still wanted that name – Nance. It belonged to me and I had earned it.

I remember sitting there waiting for my lawyer to come back to tell me my divorce was final. While I waited, I looked at the newspaper clipping of Hanslee. He looked confused and scared, but with no real emotional expression. I could not imagine how he might be feeling. The photo probably was taken before he was accused of murder. The woman he was involved with must have reported him to the police several times because the newspaper story stated that he had a history of domestic violence. I read the clipping over and over and wondered again how he could have done such a thing. The more I thought about it, the more I believed if I had stayed with him, he would have killed me. I thanked God for protecting me.

Hanslee's Call

Strange dreams about Hanslee made me anticipate his call. Sure enough, on Saturday, April 26th, 2002, at 4:20a.m., he called me. Even though I had prayed for that moment, I was surprised by his call. Somehow it seemed so surreal. I was anxious to hear his side of the story. He spoke to me in the usual familiar tone.

"Hey, Sweets," he began.

"Hey. Where are you?" I wanted to know.

"Don't worry about that," he answered. "Have you divorced me yet?" He asked in a demanding way.

"Why?" I asked. Our divorce was final in January, but I was afraid to tell him because I knew he would feel I had betrayed him. During our conversation, I started thinking about what I would do about calling the detective.

"Have the people called you to tell you what happened?" he asked.

"Yes. They said you beat somebody up and the person died. What happened? What have you done?" I questioned him.

"I entered into a room and sat down with the devil himself," he replied.

"What do you mean?" I pleaded.

"I thought I was tough but I was wrong. The devil tried to kill me... I wish I could see you again but I can't. I'm glad one of my wishes came true, I was able to talk to you one last time. I wish I could hold you and kiss you like I used to. I'm sorry for all I've done to you. God gave me an angel when He allowed you to come into my life. I didn't realize it until it was too late. I'm sorry, Sweets; divorce me and go on with your life. You deserve to be happy. This will be the last time I'll be able to talk to you."

"Where did you get my number?" I shivered with fright.

"Don't worry about that. I'm not coming to your house," he said. Then he started quoting scriptures from John, Chapter One, and Matthew 6:33 of the Holy Bible. "I've been reading these scriptures a lot lately. I believe I'm going to die soon," he continued.

"Why do you think you're going to die?"

"It's too late for me. The devil tried to kill me," he said repeatedly.

"As long as you have breath in your body, there is hope for survival. You just have to learn to trust in God."

After I hung up, I agonized over whether or not I should call the police. Would they believe me if I told them the number he called from was a blocked call? I wondered where he was and how he got my number. I also wondered if he had my address and if he was going to come to my house. I became extremely afraid.

I didn't want the detectives to think I was harboring a fugitive, so I called Detective Kalebota to tell him Hanslee had called me. I told him I was afraid because Hanslee wished he could see me once more. I thought he was going to come to my house. This made me remember another call I had received from my sister back in 2001 during the Thanksgiving holiday. It was before I knew about the murder. I began to figure out what was unfolding.

"Mother said Lee came looking for you," Loretta had informed me.

"What did he say?" I asked.

"You'll have to call Mother and ask her. He also called here for you a few times. He just asked if you were here and if I had a number to reach you," she explained.

In the past, I would be very excited to hear Hanslee was looking for me, but this time I wondered what his purpose was. What did he want? Each time I prayed to hear from him, it happened. This time I didn't know if I should have been praying for him to call me.

Back in June 2001, I had thought about going home to be near my mother because I was homesick. Then, I had a feeling that it wasn't time for me to go back. Now, thinking back, I know I made the right decision. What if I had been there when he was looking for me? I could see myself falling for his lies. I doubt he would have told me what he had done, or what he was accused of doing. I could see him trying to apologize and convincing me we belonged together. I could see myself looking for a place for us to live and starting all over again. The thought was scary after knowing the truth. Thank God I'd had a premonition not to go back.

On April 27th I received several calls from Hanslee and it sounded like he was in Kansas. I thought he was on his way to my house. I called Detective Kalebota and left him a message that Hanslee had called me again and I was afraid he would come to my house.

The last call I received from Hanslee was later that night. He kept telling me to hold on. It sounded like he would lay the phone down and leave the room for a few minutes. "Are you still there?" he would ask each time he came back to the phone.

"Hold on a minute, somebody's knocking at the door," I said at one point. I was lying across my bed while talking to him. I got up to see who was at the door. It was two Lenexa police officers.

"Who else is in the home with you? Is Hanslee here?" the female officer asked.

"My two sons are here, and no, Hanslee is not here," I replied. "But he is on the phone." I motioned to the officer to follow me into my bedroom and I handed her my cordless phone for her to listen. I did that so she wouldn't think I was hiding Hanslee in my apartment.

She took the phone and whispered, "Get him to tell you where he is."

"Where are you?" I asked Hanslee.

"The less you know, the less you'll have to say," he replied. "I'm not going to hunt you down. I could get your address if I wanted to. Did the police come back out looking for me?"

"No, but they probably will contact me and I will have to tell them you called me," I answered.

"I want to see you one more time, but I'm not coming to Kansas," he assured me. Then he started saying something about the devil, piranhas and messing with the wrong people. I could barely understand what he was talking about. "There's no hope for me. I had to fight for my life. Nothing can be done for me now."

I tried to encourage him not to give up, but he was not listening to me. He seemed paranoid, and acted as if he was in his own little world.

This incident and the statement I gave to Detective Kalebota about Hanslee's first call in November were in the discovery. Later, Hanslee sent me a nasty letter along with his discovery. In Detective Kalebota's report, Hanslee circled what he felt I had lied about. I was hurt that he thought I had betrayed him, but he had made up his mind that I should never have been talking to "those people."

The Nasty Letter

TO: Darlene

FROM:

STREET:

CITY:

STATE:

How are you doing I guess you are doing just fine Now consider the position that I'm in. Thanks to you! you know I told you that I was going to turn myself in when I got some money for a lawyer. No! but you told to do make a dam dicision about my life Darlene. Not yours! But Maybe you understand My

My Life Not Yours

And Then you took up on your self to even lie to these people And you told Them That I said I Had to do What I Had to do You Are A Dam Lie

And the Type of
Person you are you would
Rather see me spend the
Rest of my life in Jail
Long As you knew That
I wasn't At Being Happy
With some One Else Any
decision you have made for
me have been no good
So what the hell would make
you think that I would Tell
you else something such As
you lied you Lied
you Lied
you Are A Dam Lie

you Dam Lie

TO:
FROM:
STREET:
CITY:
STATE:

AND WHERE IN
the hell does
your stupid ass
get off on tellin
me that I'm
in jail

And you said that
you need to talk
to me well what in
the hell do you want
to talk to me about

you want to tell me you ④
are going to get me A Lawyer
No! your not going to tell
me THAT   And No!
you can't send me two
PHONE Card Because its
Not Allowed Here
I do Not STANd
A CHANCE With A
State Appointed LAwyer
you do Not Have The
slightest Idea About The LAw
so How IN THe Hell Are
you goin to make A
decision WITH my Life
you Lied

TO: WHAT you WANT to
FROM: talk to me ABOUt
STREET:
CITY: DARlene. That you
STATE:

ARE SORRy I AM Not
only Not tryiNN To HER
I AiN't HERE?N I ,
DARleNE you HAv got
life AND BUllSh:t
Mixed UP

you lied you lied
WHAt WERE you wanting
To Tell me DARleNE
Some more bad News

Is THAT WHAT you WANT ⑪
to tell me THAT you
got some Body else
Well I guess you
Would WAIT UNTIL I WAS
IN HERE OR dead so
you wouldn't have to WORRY
ABout me Being HAPPY
WITH some one else other THAN
you

I got my Discovery papers
IN Aug. It's something THAT tells
everything such As you skank Lie
I WAS WONDERing WHAT you WERE
Talking ABout WHEN you wrote me THE
First Time WHEN you said THAT
you didn't Know WHAT to say I see
Why NoW you LIAR YOU DAM
LIE

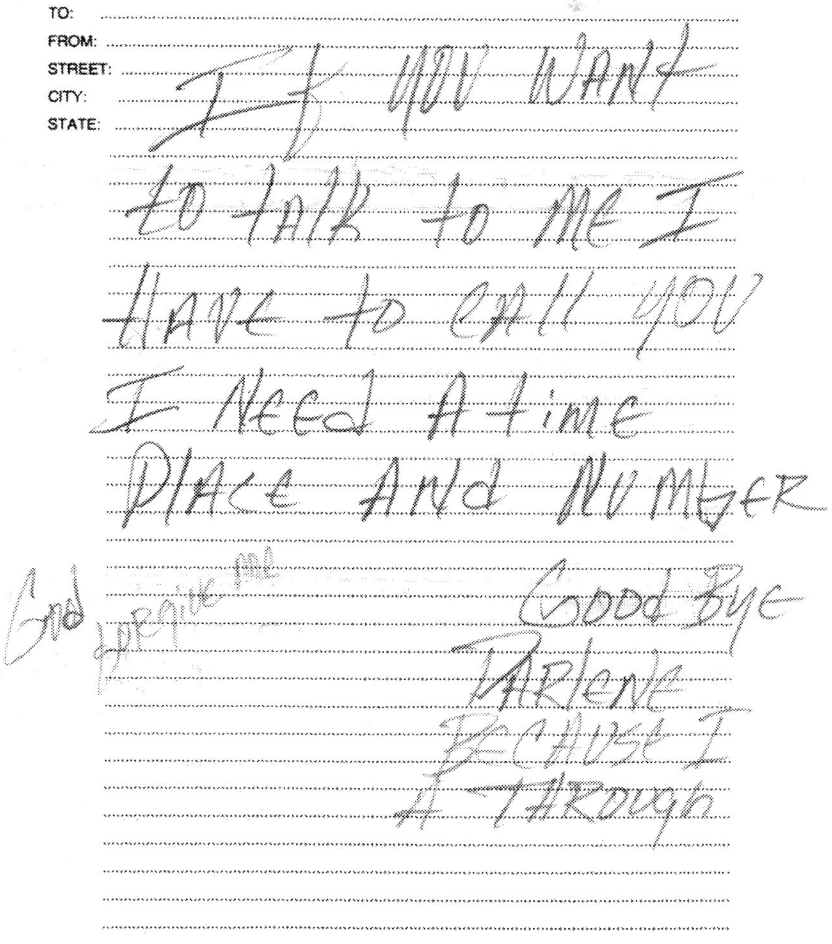

TO:

FROM:

STREET:

CITY:

STATE:

If you want
to talk to me I
Have to call you
I Need A time
Place And Number

God
forgive me

Good Bye
Darlene
Because I
A Through

Sometime in April 2002, Hanslee was picked up as a suspect in the murder of his ex-girlfriend. After that, he began writing to me. The first few letters were nice ones. But all of a sudden, I received a very nasty letter, postmarked March 17, 2003. He was extremely upset with me.

I was exhausted after I read this letter from Hanslee. At first, the things he said made me feel like it was partly my fault. But, when I thought about it more, I realized he was still trying to abuse me, even from behind bars.

I responded to his letter in an attempt to defend myself. I wanted him to know I didn't remember him telling me he was going to turn himself in, and that "those people" must have twisted my words. I told him that he couldn't blame me because the police picked him up. I also explained that Josh knew he was in jail because he had heard a few of my family members discussing it.

His letter also surprised me with yet another mind game attempting to put me on the defense by saying I wanted to write him with "bad news" that I had someone else. This came out of left field. I had no idea what he was talking about, as I had not been in any other relationship.

There were times I thought about what would happen when Hanslee got released from jail. Would he try to contact me to tell me he was sorry, or to tell me he hated me for telling the police he had called me? The thought of him getting out still haunts me. I once saw a special on television about a young man who got out of jail and killed his own brother because he testified in the case against him. He also killed several kids who witnessed him killing his brother. Even though these thoughts pass through my mind, I encourage myself by believing that God's angels are watching over me.

After he didn't respond to my letter, I realized I really didn't have to explain anything to him. I also realized that by trying to explain, I was being drawn back into that cycle again: he blames me, I feel guilty, he's satisfied. I had to remind myself I had made a decision when I left him – I was not going to allow him to abuse me anymore, not even from a distance. It didn't matter what I said or didn't say to "those people," it was **his** fault he ended up in jail.

I became very upset when I received the police report (which Hanslee sent to me) and discovered it included my address. I couldn't believe the County Prosecutor's office did not protect my personal information. It seemed to me that they were defeating their purpose when they put one person's life at stake in the process of prosecuting a criminal for taking another person's life. Some prosecutors take more extreme measures to protect their witnesses, but they did not in Hanslee's case. Later, when the detective informed me that I was going to be a witness for the prosecution, the idea that Hanslee had my personal address became a major concern for me, because the thought of him coming to Kansas looking for me was dreadful. My belief in the protection of God's angels helped me get past this dreadful thought.

Finding New Meaning for My Life

By August 2002 homesickness and Bradrell's defiant behavior drove me back to Baton Rouge. Several weeks before we left Kansas, Bradrell threatened to hit me. Bradrell was hanging out with friends I didn't approve of. I demanded he come home, but he showed up two days later. I guess he had spent the night with his friend Carlton. I was sitting at my computer working on my homework when he came in the front door. I turned and looked him square in the eyes and said, "You are grounded." He ignored me and continued walking to his room.

One of his friends came in behind him. "Hello, Ms. Dunn," he said, and followed Bradrell to his room. When they came out Bradrell had a white Wal-Mart bag with some clothes in it as if he was leaving again.

"I meant what I said. You're grounded," I insisted.

"I don't care," he replied, and proceeded to walk out the door.

"You are not going anywhere," I said as I grabbed his arm. He pulled away from me and drew his hand back as if he was going to hit me.

"It's not worth it, man," said his friend.

I walked to my room. My heart was racing, but I was more hurt than afraid. I could not believe what had just happened. I paced a few times around my room, and then picked up a plastic pole about 15 inches around and 4 feet long that was part of Josh's basketball goal. I felt it would take more than a belt to put Bradrell in his place. He was 15 at the time, weighed 155 pounds, and stood 5'10". By the time I walked back to the living room he had left. This gave me the chance to calm down and think about what to do next.

As tears rolled down my face I realized I didn't want to use violence to control my child. I wished my love for him was enough to keep him from becoming like his father and stepfather. I put the pole down on the chair, went back into my room, picked up the phone and called the police. I knew I needed help controlling my son. When they arrived, I told them my son had threatened to hit me.

Bradrell was standing outside the front door, and the policeman asked, "Are you Bradrell Dunn?"

"Yes," he replied.

They handcuffed him and took him to JDC, a place for juvenile delinquents. When I went to visit him, he didn't seem to care about anything, not even the consequences of his actions. He showed no emotion at all, but said to me, "I just want to do my time and get out of here."

So, he did his time and came home with an "I don't care" attitude. I didn't know what else to do. I was overwhelmed with the fact that I didn't have my family or anyone to help me deal with my child. I loved him very much and wanted the best for him, but I didn't seem to have the answers. This incident really had a lot to do with my decision to go back home. I knew I wouldn't have to worry about running into Hanslee, because he was no longer there. I had planned to pick up where I left off, but things don't always turn out the way you plan.

I moved in with Loretta until I could find my own place. But by the time I found something, frustration had already set in, and I wanted to go back to Kansas. I will admit, it was nice to move across the street from my sister. The house was a three-bedroom home with a large front yard and fenced-in backyard, as well as a covered carport. The bathroom and kitchen were big and roomy, and the living room was nice and comfortable.

But something was different. I couldn't stop thinking about all the things that had changed since I returned home. There were drug dealers hanging out on the corner by my sister's house. I was afraid that since Bradrell was still upset with me for moving to Baton Rouge, he would eventually join them.

After I called the police to report the drug dealers, they busted down my back door. The drug dealer also beat up Bradrell. Bradrell told us it was because they wanted the money he had stolen from a convenience store. I asked Bradrell why he had robbed the store, but he wouldn't tell me the whole story. I figured he was just being rebellious.

I couldn't find a decent job, and had to return to my old job – working the graveyard shift at a printing factory making $7.50 an hour. It was hard trying to live on this pay, and I was miserable.

Realizing that life at home couldn't be like it once was, with Loretta and my mother taking care of me like old times, I decided it was time to take care of my children, take my chances, and return to Kansas. This was another sad time for my family; they hated to see me leave again. Bradrell, Hanslee III, and Josh had already started school, but that didn't stop me. All of my kids wanted to stay in Baton Rouge, but only Bradrell was allowed to stay. He liked the school he attended, and Loretta wouldn't have to find a babysitter for him because he was 15.

I was glad to be back in Kansas, even though we had to sleep in the car for a night or two. After I tried the homeless hotline number for the third time, I was given information about an opening at a shelter in the northeast area of Kansas City, Missouri. After we were accepted, I was able to give my kids and myself a bath. The shelter gave us hot meals and beds to sleep in every night until my application for an apartment was approved. Even though we couldn't stay at the shelter during the day, it was much safer than sleeping in my car. I still felt very blessed. My kids seemed to be happy, too. The only time they complained was when we had to wait for the shelter to open at 6 p.m. each day.

Finally we moved into our own apartment. I was ready to settle down and have a normal life, and made plans to return to school. I wasn't worried about not having any furniture; I was confident I would get some when I received the key to my apartment. The apartment manager was very kind to me. I told her my story and it was to my surprise that she had been through a similar situation. She said, "I left my husband because he abused me also." She allowed me to move in without paying the security deposit. The help she gave me made a big difference in my life. God always put the right people in my path during my unpredictable journey.

When I went to the apartment complex to sign my lease, the manager told me two detectives had come looking for me several times. She gave me Detective Kalebota's business card. He was the detective in New Jersey. He wanted me to call, but I didn't because I couldn't handle anymore interruptions or problems in my life. The following week I moved into my apartment. It didn't take much to enroll Hanslee, Josh, and myself back into school.

Everything was going great for us until Hanslee III started to act up in school. His teachers reported he was not cooperating with them, and he was not performing up to his potential. He got so rebellious with me and his teachers that I sent him to Boys Town for eighteen months. He had begun staying out until two or three o'clock in the morning, smoking pot, and hanging out with the other rebellious kids in the neighborhood. It turned out to be a good thing for Hanslee to go to Boys Town; another miracle from God. I didn't have to worry about where he was at night, and he learned how to redirect his life in a positive way.

After getting Hanslee placed at Boys Town, I met with Josh's teacher and realized he was struggling in school. Because of all the moving from place to place, my kids were having a hard time adjusting to each change. I blamed myself. I felt bad when Josh's teacher suggested he be placed in the learning center, a class that helped slow kids. I agreed at first, but later I insisted Josh be taken out of the learning center because he was falling further and further behind his classmates. This had happened to Hanslee III previously. I was too busy trying to please his father and allowed Hanslee III to fall through the educational cracks, giving educators permission to label him "learning disabled." I was determined not to let it happen to Josh.

I love Josh's determination. He never liked being in the learning center. He said, "I don't want to go to the LC room; I want to stay in class like everyone else."

I suggested he write a letter to his teacher. He wrote the letter and the teacher called me the next day. "Let's try it," she said. Josh ended up being able to perform academically well along with the other children. I was so proud of him!

The ordeal with Hanslee III and Josh was behind me. I thought about how exciting it was to be back in school. I had enjoyed my past experience at UMKC. It was great to learn new and enlightening things. I had purchased all my school supplies and was ready to start my classes. I never thought I would have to face another obstacle so soon. The detective from the New Jersey police department was still trying to contact me.

One day in October 2003, as I was checking my mailbox and getting into my car, the apartment manager pulled up beside me.

"They're waiting for you in my office," she said in a concerned way.

"Who?" I inquired curiously.

"The detectives from New Jersey, they said if you don't meet them now, they will go down to your kid's school."

"Give me a minute; tell them I'll be right there," I requested of her. I went to my apartment to drop off my mail, then walked back to the office to meet with them. Josh and Hanslee III were in school, and Bradrell was still in Louisiana. What could they want with me? My heart pounded with nervousness. I can't go to New Jersey, I thought; my classes start next week. I never thought I would have to be involved in Hanslee's trial. I thought as long as I wasn't harboring him, I wouldn't have to participate anymore. I walked on into the office.

"My name is Detective Kalebota and this is Detective O'Neill," one of the officers greeted me. They wanted a statement from me concerning the homicide case against my ex-husband.

The office manager allowed us to use the clubhouse to conduct the interview. I answered all of their questions, hoping I would never have to see them again or go to New Jersey. I was nervous the whole time, and expressed to the detectives my fear that Hanslee would get out of jail, hunt me down, and punish me for giving a statement. Somehow, I thought my statement would incriminate him. But I knew that if he had done what they said, he should suffer the consequences. They assured me Hanslee was not getting out. "We have his confession on tape," Detective Kalebota said. So I told the truth about Hanslee's treatment of me.

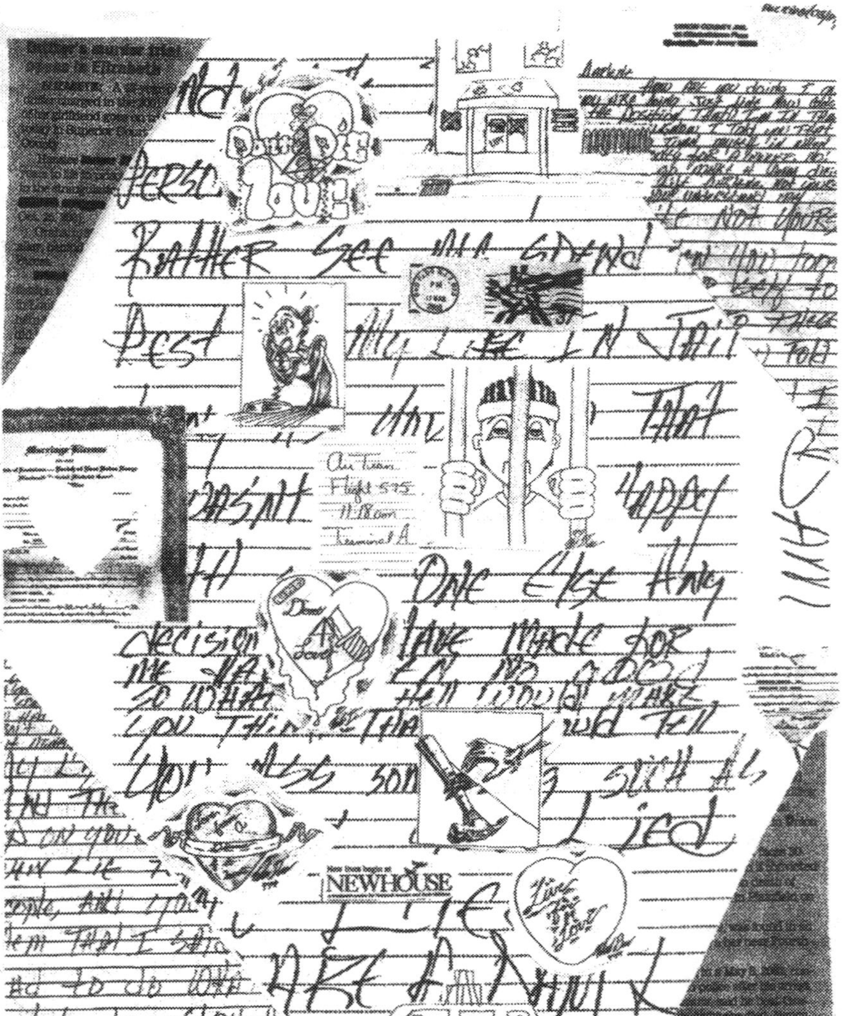

The Trip to New Jersey

On May 18th, 2004, at about 7:30p.m., there was a knock at my apartment door. Josh opened the door.

"Someone has left you a note," said Deb, my neighbor, as she handed it to me.

I was surprised, but unfolded the note and read it:

Darlene,
Det. Oliver Kalebota called.
He would like you to call him.

I called him first thing the next morning. "What's going on with Hanslee's case?" I asked.

"He wants to go to court. We need you to come to New Jersey to testify as a character witness. We will be asking you about the statement you gave us last October," he explained. I almost passed out. I could not believe this was happening. I thought it was over; I never thought I would have to deal with Hanslee again.

By the beginning of June that year, Bradrell (now 16 years old) had returned from Baton Rouge for a week, and Hanslee III (14) was home from Boys Town for a week. Josh was 8 at the time. On June 5th, the four of us boarded an airplane, bound for New Jersey. When I first found out we would need to fly, I was afraid. But once we were on our way, I felt brave. The day was cloudy and slightly foggy, but the trip to the airport was pleasant. My sons and I were on a plane for the first time and on our way to New Jersey.

As we waited for the plane to take off, I noticed the rain drops on the windowpane. I finally accepted the fact that the trip would make a difference. Up in the sky, 34,000 feet about the beautiful clouds, I realized we were actually flying. The clouds looked like a sea of pure white cotton. I felt wonderful even though I had stepped outside my comfort zone. I never thought I would step foot on an airplane, but now the phrase "never say never" meant something. The experience was out of this world.

Detective Kalebota was waiting for us when we arrived. He shook my hand, and then each of my sons', as he introduced himself. He was so nice; he reminded me of the white guy who played in the television show *Miami Vice*.

Two days later, I was still in New Jersey, waiting in our hotel room to testify at Hanslee's trial. I was anxious for this ordeal to be over, but was also enjoying the hospitality. It was nice not having to clean up or cook. The food was great, and the kids really enjoyed watching cable television because we didn't have it at home. We all had fun swimming in the hotel pool.

Finally, the phone rang. It was Prosecutor Donnelly calling. "Can you meet me downstairs in the lobby?" he asked.

"Yes," I answered. It took me a few minutes to change, having just come in from the pool, but I hurried to meet him.

Kalebota and Donnelly were sitting in the dining area of the hotel, so I joined them. "Is everything going okay?" Donnelly asked. "How are you? How are the kids?" He was a tall, fair man with average build and dark hair. He looked like Brad on *The Young and the Restless*, I thought.

"Everything's going okay. We just finished swimming. I'm doing okay, and the kids are getting used to the idea of being here," I told him.

"We would like to go over some questions Donnelly will be asking you tomorrow," said Kalebota.

I was anxious for the whole thing to be over. The more questions they asked the more tense I became.

"What do you remember about the phone conversation with Hanslee?" Donnelly asked.

"Just that he called to say goodbye, that he loved me, and wouldn't ever see me again. I asked him why, and told him that the police were looking for him and saying that he had beaten someone to death. When I asked him what he had done, he said he didn't do anything," I told Donnelly.

"Did you ask him if the person was a woman?" Donnelly wanted to know.

"I don't remember," I said. I began to get stressed because I couldn't remember exactly what was said. I mentioned that I was writing a book. I hadn't meant to bring that up, but happened to think that I might have the answer to his question in my notes.

"Do you have any of that with you?" Donnelly asked.

"Yes. I'll be right back," I replied and went up to my room.

It was getting late and the kids were complaining that they were hungry. I took the notes back down to the detectives and told them, "The kids are asking for something to eat. I will have to go order them something while you look over the notes."

But Donnelly had to leave, so he said, "We will be back tomorrow. Continue looking over the statement you gave Kalebota. Look for more notes concerning this case, anything you wrote between 2001 and 2002. We need that stuff. It is important you give us everything you have." Then they left.

The next day, Kalebota picked up the kids and me and took us to the county prosecutor's office. I was hoping the kids would have a chance to see Hanslee; Josh really wanted to see his dad. But the prosecutor said the kids would stay in the office while we were at the courthouse.

A support staff at the prosecutor's office led my kids to the video games. Detective Kalebota, Detective Furda (who was assisting with the case) and I walked to the courthouse, located a couple of blocks from the prosecutor's office. When we arrived at the courthouse Detective Kalebota joined the prosecutor in the courtroom. I had to wait for about an hour to testify, and was a nervous wreck. I sat on a hard wooden bench outside the courtroom, watching people going in and out.

"Hello," said a man beside me.

"Hi," I replied.

"I don't understand why Hanslee has gotten himself into this mess," continued the man.

"I don't either," I responded, hoping he would not ask me any questions about who I was or anything about the case. I wished I didn't have to be there. I felt like I was betraying Hanslee in some way. I had already decided to forgive him for what he had done to me. But by testifying, I felt I wasn't showing him that I had forgiven him. Then again, I felt in another way that I was doing the right thing; that if he had killed someone, he should suffer the consequences of his actions. I had to realize my testimony wouldn't cause him to go to prison. If he went to prison, it would be because the evidence proved him guilty.

Finally it was my turn to testify. As I walked to the stand, I couldn't take my eyes off Hanslee. He had gained a lot of weight, and his skin was pale, as if he hadn't had any sun for a while. He looked at me as if he were okay with me being there. His lips read, "Hey, Sweets." He looked so innocent.

After I took the oath, Donnelly asked me if I could identify Hanslee. He asked me some of the same questions Kalebota had asked me in October 2002.

At one point Hanslee's attorney objected to the line of questioning. Donnelly wrote the word "HURT" on a piece of paper and showed it to me. I noticed Hanslee leaning over toward his attorney to say something to him.

"Does this bring back any memory of the conversation you had with Hanslee on the night he called you?" he asked, referring to the word on the paper.

"No," I said without thinking.

But my mind continued to work on that word, HURT, and I began to remember something. I had previously told Donnelly that Hanslee had said some more people were going to get hurt. Now I didn't know what to do with this sudden memory. I had already said no, and I didn't want the court to think I was lying under oath, so I said nothing about what I had just remembered.

"No further questions," Donnelly stated. I walked out of the courtroom wondering if my kids or I would ever see Hanslee again.

The Verdict

On June 24th, 2004, Hanslee III told me, "The police from New Jersey called."

"What did they say?" I asked.

"He was convicted," he replied as he walked out the door.

"Oh, no!" I cried. My heart began to hurt all over again. I didn't want to believe Hanslee was a murderer.

I called my mother later that day to tell her about Hanslee. She was just as dismayed as I was. We were surprised and saddened that the father of two of my children and become abusive *to the point of actually killing someone.* It was hard to believe that ***I had almost died for love.*** Mother encouraged me, saying, "Don't let it get to you or make you depressed. Just thank God it wasn't you." But it made me so sad that Hanslee had thrown his life away.

Hanslee, like anyone else, had a choice. We all have choices: we can choose life, or we can choose death. He chose drugs and violence, which is death. He could have chosen life – **the Lord Jesus Christ**.

Even though I had cared for Hanslee, I have chosen to live my life walking with God. Therefore, there is no place in my life for someone who has chosen death. I will continue to pray God's blessings on Hanslee, because he is my children's father, but our relationship is over.

THE END

Living for Love

I have chosen to live for love. I'm so proud of myself as a single parent because I'm providing for my children's needs. I am glad I am alive to see my children grow up. I pray they will become strong black men who will work hard to achieve their goals and give back to their community.

I am proud to be a member of Lenexa Christian Center, and God is using me in positive ways. I sponsor an orphan child named Isaac who lives in Kenya. He wants to go to college to become a teacher.

I have received an Associate Degree in Liberal Arts with an emphasis in Accounting, and am working on my Bachelor's Degree. I also received a Certificate of Graduation for completing Dimensions – Career Path and Job Search Modules program at the Women's Employment Network (WEN). I was nervous about getting back into the workforce, but the WEN program taught me to have confidence and helped me recognize my strengths. I currently have a wonderful job which has helped me graduate from the County Housing Family Self-Sufficiency Program and to get off welfare assistance.

Even though I have moved 900 miles away from my family, I call them almost every day and visit every chance I get. I am currently working on writing a documentary about my entire family.

WHEN I LOVE MYSELF

When I love myself
I'm at peace with God

When I love myself
I know who I am and Whose I am

When I love myself
I am no longer bound

I can speak with authority
Because I know my words will have meaning

When I love myself
I do not allow others to dictate who I am
I also set boundaries

When I love myself I am free

Eva Howard, MSW, LCSW, LSCSW

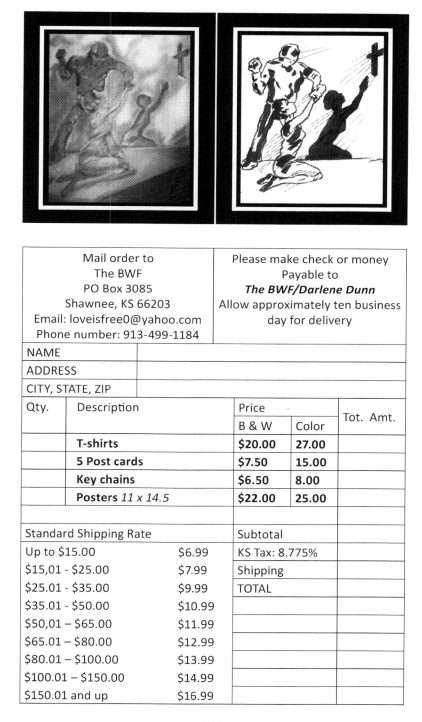

Cut Here

Mail order to The BWF PO Box 3085 Shawnee, KS 66203 Email: loveisfree0@yahoo.com Phone number: 913-499-1184		Please make check or money Payable to ***The BWF/Darlene Dunn*** Allow approximately ten business day for delivery		
NAME				
ADDRESS				
CITY, STATE, ZIP				
Qty.	Description	Price		Tot. Amt.
		B & W	Color	
	T-shirts	**$20.00**	**27.00**	
	5 Post cards	**$7.50**	**15.00**	
	Key chains	**$6.50**	**8.00**	
	Posters *11 x 14.5*	**$22.00**	**25.00**	
Standard Shipping Rate		Subtotal		
Up to $15.00	$6.99	KS Tax: 8.775%		
$15,01 - $25.00	$7.99	Shipping		
$25.01 - $35.00	$9.99	TOTAL		
$35.01 - $50.00	$10.99			
$50,01 – $65.00	$11.99			
$65.01 – $80.00	$12.99			
$80.01 – $100.00	$13.99			
$100.01 – $150.00	$14.99			
$150.01 and up	$16.99			

163